LUKAS & STERNBERG, NEW YORK 002

JEROEN DE RIJKE / WILLEM DE ROOIJ
AFTER THE HUNT

LUKAS *&* STERNBERG, NEW YORK

Jeroen de Rijke/Willem de Rooij

After the Hunt

Publisher/Verlag: Lukas & Sternberg, New York

Edition/Auflage: 2000

© 2000 Lukas & Sternberg, Frankfurter Kunstverein, Museum Abteiberg, Authors and Artists

Exhibitions/Ausstellungen: Frankfurter Kunstverein, May 28 - July 11, 1999

Städtisches Museum Abteiberg, Mönchengladbach, May 29 - July 4, 1999

Editors/Herausgeber: Veit Loers, Nicolaus Schafhausen, Caroline Schneider

Translation/Übersetzung: Robert Hardwick-Weston, Kristina Jensen, Andrew Lederer-Homan,

Allison Plath-Moseley, Nicolaus Schafhausen

Copy Editor/Lektor: Meg O'Rourke, Hortense Pisano, Allison Plath-Moseley, Paul Rieder

Design/Gestaltung: Markus Weisbeck, Ingrid Haug, Frankfurt am Main

Printing and binding/Druck und Bindung: Berlin, Germany

Supported by the Mondriaan Foundation, Ambassade van het Koninkrijk der Nederlanden, Berlin

ISBN 0-9671802-0-1

Lukas & Sternberg Inc.

1182 Broadway # 1602

New York, NY 10001

e-mail: l-s@thing.net

CONTENTS / INHALT

IF ONLY ALL ROOMS WOULD SO CLEARLY FULFILL THEIR PURPOSE...

NICOLAUS SCHAFHAUSEN: You demand a great deal from the public: only those who have continually wrestled with the conflict between "what should I see" – "what do I actually see" are able to understand the mechanism of representation and conditioned perception.

Don't these didactic production methods contradict the way art has been understood in the last few years? Isn't the viewer expected to make more of a "Eigenleistung" (personal contribution), to be free to interpret?

The dramaturgy in your films is disturbing, since perception constantly has the urge to make connections. That means, you force the viewer – I'd like to say – into a corset, limiting his possibilities of perception. Is it necessary to educate the viewer? "May" he only think about what you give him?

JEROEN DE RIJKE/WILLEM DE ROOIJ: We decide on the meaning of a piece first, and then we choose its form. If we decide on the form first, it's because we like its meaning. But mostly, we like a form because of its beauty.

We just like order. We feel the greatest possible intellectual and spiritual freedom by watching, for instance, a piece by Judd, or Vermeer, or Stanley Brouwn – artists who work in an extremely defined formal grid. But between the lines of this grid there are huge empty spaces... We're not expressionist artists. We calculate every step we take very precisely, and we trust that the gaps in our grid provide space for the viewers.

Though our pieces are not meant to be meditative, as many people seem to think, they do deal with meditative issues. In the practice of Zen meditation, a set of rigid rules of behavior – followed to the extent that one experiences physical pain – will ultimately provide mental space.

We like to stand in a museum and watch a painting. We like conventional ways of showing and watching a 2D piece. The act of watching is important to us, and the way the viewer and the projection are situated in front of each other is part of the installation. There are plenty of possibilities for free interpretation within the frame, but we like to show our pieces in a room that has only one function: confrontation with, and, if needed, contemplation of a piece of art. If only all rooms would so clearly fulfill their purpose...

There's plenty of room for "Eigenleistung" in our work, within the limits we propose. Interactivity is definitely not for us.

To us, an art piece is an art piece, and a viewer is a viewer. We find the distance created by this construction very pleasant. The viewer doesn't have to finish our pieces; they don't have any influence on them because they are not artists.

We've heard about this wish for free interpretation as a key to nineties art, though. We never really understood why. Why should a viewer not be satisfied any more with merely looking at something? We think the act of looking (at our work) is enough of a "Eigenleistung" in itself.

Another word often heard is generous. This obviously means that an artist should give and give and give, and make the public feel good – good about themselves and their interpretative skills – and the artist should be witty, smart, and friendly. But an artist is not a social worker, nor an event broker, and an art piece doesn't have to be nice. It's OK for a viewer to work a bit. It doesn't always have to be nice.

The formal grids we work with, inside and outside the image are, like any grid, quite abstract. It seems many young artists find abstract art "too elitist", and think art should be taken out of the institutions as soon as possible, in order to make it more accessible for a larger public. This is the opposite of our views. We don't object to art being elitist. As a matter of fact, we love the fact that it's elitist. We're not creating a mass product, and we're not democratic. Of course, this doesn't mean that we always like the public we get. Maybe every artist dreams of his ideal public. Not every person who happens to have the money and time to be able to walk into a library or a museum is an intelligent viewer. It's important for museums and galleries to be accessible to people from different social and economical situations.

Every artist makes decisions in his work. It would be quite strange to assume that one decision is more imperative to the viewer than another. Every viewer probably has his own hang-up. Personally, our problem is that we feel very forced when we have the feeling that an artist wants us to "feel free...". It's like meeting a stranger who'll tell you all about himself and then say to you, "Oh, listen to me, I'm just rambling on. Now tell me about yourself!" What are you supposed to say? We would need a more specific question to be able to come up with an answer.

We don't make a piece with an audience in mind. Maybe, in the end, we're not even that interested in what the public thinks.

N. SCH.: In your most recent film, *Of Three Men*, the theme is an exploration of the concept of a "cultural location" that uses a specific "concrete location". I find this the most impressive of your films so far, because it fundamentally questions the increasing homogenization that seems to be a by-product of the so-called "cultural globalization".

What motivated you to take a Neo-Romanesque church in Amsterdam, which today is used as a mosque, and make it the subject matter of your film?

D. RI./D. RO.: We were looking for a mosque. We'd seen some beautiful mosques in Istanbul and the proportions of those spaces impressed us. We're used to our Christian altar being at the end of a rectangular, tunnel-like space. A mosque is square, and feels more spacious, also because there are no benches. Not only is there space for other things like light and scale, but you also don't have to look at all those useless ugly things that surround us in daily life.

Praying in a direction (east) evokes a much larger feeling than praying to a central focus point, such as a cross. We also liked the prohibition of image, and that all decoration should be abstract in a mosque, and that those repeating abstract patterns are supposed to make you think of God. In our fantasy, we made a mix between the mosque and the white cube decorated with its modern painting, because we loved to think about empty white spaces with abstract surfaces in them. Of course, all this changed when we found the Fatih mosque, because it didn't look like a white cube, but instead, like a Saenredam painting we both like a lot, *De St. Odolphuskerk te Assendelft*. Saenredam's paintings try to evoke the divine spirit through the rigid rules of perspective. Human figures seem to serve merely to emphasize the huge, unshakeable space that surrounds them. We were glad to find a mosque that was, or had been, a church – although it changed our plans and the content of the film dramatically.

N. SCH.: By presenting the methods of perception belonging to two competing societal models, are you also trying to show the impossibility of unifying geographic contexts?

D. RI./D. RO.: Cultures are strong. People will hold on to them for a long time. It's clearly visible in the Surinamian population in Amsterdam. In Surinam, several different ethnic groups lived together for hundreds of years. There were the South American Indians (the original inhabitants), the Creoles (brought from Ghana on slave ships by Dutch colonists in the 17th century), the Chinese, the Javanese (imported by the Dutch from their other colony, Indonesia), the Hindus (imported from India as contract laborers), and, of course, the Dutch. After Surinam gained its independence in 1975, many inhabitants chose to live in Holland. The *Hindustanen* and the Indians in Amsterdam buy their food in the same shops, and they rent their *Bollywood* films in the same specialized video stores. Recent research proved that the Creole and Ghanaian populations in Amsterdam also still share many habits.

People are obviously so flexible that they find ways to continue their habits and rituals even under extreme circumstances and after drastic changes of cultural and geographical surroundings. Maybe the film shows that these processes can lead to some very peculiar hybrid results. We see them everywhere.

What the film doesn't show is daily reality in Amsterdam. People have found a way to more or less peacefully coexist (although lately, especially Moroccan teenagers have been in revolt, out of dissatisfaction with their situation), but mutual integration between the Dutch and the other 50 percent of the city seldom works. One of the biggest problems the city will be facing within ten years is the increasing formation of black schools, where students rapidly fall behind in Dutch language, with disastrous consequences for their future.

N. SCH.: Then does the film also imply that we can indeed exist together in a geographic space, but that life itself is only possible in chatrooms?

D. RI./D. RO.: It seems natural that your own chatroom will be the first one you visit, even when you're in another country. We lived in and around Bombay for six months and met only filmmakers. The fact that you move to another country doesn't mean you suddenly start socializing with plumbers or cowherds. You also don't do so at home.

Of course, you can meet people from other chatrooms, but that will mean a lot of translation problems (even if you speak the same language), and a lot of energy and time; and we frankly believe that most people are just not prepared to take all that trouble. People have always lived in chatrooms. Maybe it's a problem for some people that at the moment, the different chatrooms are becoming more diverse, yet smaller. Maybe people who worry too much about globalization spend too much time in their own social circles – their own chatrooms, wherever in the world. We think that if any one of them would spend a month with a family that, for instance, earns half or double his income, or has a strong religious background of some kind, then he would have a much clearer sense of difference, even if he were in his own city.

We think this globalization trauma simply sprouts from visiting too many airports, and we think there's even a lot of difference between those. The fact that there are more visible similarities between different locations does not mean that the differences have disappeared – they've just shifted to other places. They became subtler, we think. We're interested in subtle differences, nuances.

We went to Greenland to shoot *I'm Coming Home in Forty Days*. At first glance, the land seems quite austere, containing very few ingredients: rocks, moss, sky, water, and ice. But upon closer inspection, this moss turns out to be millions of different types of moss, and the ice never looks the same because it reflects the water, and the water reflects the sky. A drifting iceberg can suddenly turn around and become a complete stranger. All of these facets can only be seen when time is invested.

Everything becomes subtler, more detailed, and more specialized. An old hit will be remixed, and become a hit again. Then the remix will be remixed. In this way, the emphasis is entirely on the similarities – and thus also on the differences – to the previous remix. But a good remix should have a good beat. If it's not catchy any more, it will be updated to suit the tastes of the day. One could say that all the songs sound the same, and that the remix is the same as the original. But that's such strange thing to say, because they're two different things – even if it's a bad remix! In the end, the star turns out to be the one who makes the remix, i.e., the one who reorganizes existing material, he who combines. In the art world, this person is the curator.

Maybe there are even more differences than before, but they're smaller. When differences become smaller, or shift to another place, one has to search for them again. But it's too easy to say they're not there. We think it's burned out and cynical to assume differences disappear. It just shows you can't see precisely, or you're too lazy to try.

N. SCH.: Doesn't the film also show that it's impossible to unprejudicially separate differing ways of life from the authors and recipients? That is, doesn't the film state that the current communication problem is actually the differing ways of communication?

D. RI./D. RO.: Yes, many of the difficulties people face in pluricultural societies, such as Amsterdam, sprout from extensive translation and communication problems. But this is not visible in the film. Among other things, the film deals with two cultures meeting in an unexpected location, the beauty and strangeness of that meeting, and the architectural extravaganza that it results in.

N. SCH.: Your film locations are always outside the everyday experience of someone who's been socialized in the West. That is, the selected locations are withdrawn from the ordinary and therefore artificial per se. Do you want to point out that everything can be exotic? Isn't this attitude too moralizing?

D. RI./D. RO.: It depends on what you mean by exotic. Linking exotic to morality implies a colonial reading of the word; it's strongly connected to guilt. That's not what we're after. We're not trying to be either politically correct or incorrect. There's no morality in any of our works. But if we used only white actors, our work would deal with whiteness; or if we shot only in the Netherlands, our work would be about being Dutch, etc. We don't think of people or locations that way.

When it comes to the exotic, we use different and sometimes ambivalent angles. When we filmed outside our daily surroundings, we tried to make images that look like they could have been made anywhere. We didn't want to make a film about India, and we had to go there to make that clear. When we filmed in the Netherlands, we used very exotic, but specifically Dutch locations: the botanical gardens in Amsterdam (a nineteenth-century Dutch vision of a tropical landscape) and the butterfly garden of the zoo in Emmen (a nineteen-seventies' Dutch vision of a rain forest). This botanical garden is as Dutch as a canal, because it sprouts from the same mind. We like the fact that these gardens are images, almost like pictures.

In his book *Infelicities*, Peter Mason beautifully explains the exotic. He describes the exotic object as a product of one culture being transported, taken out of context, and reinterpreted by another culture. This is a process of "exotification". "The exotic is never at home", he states. It's misunderstood in the culture it's been transported to, and it doesn't exist in its place of origin, because people don't regard it as exotic. We like this image of the exotic as a blank, floating thing that belongs nowhere. Anyway, we see exotic and artificial as two different things.

Our images don't come from daily life. They come from fantasies, or from other images. When we have an image in our head, we search for a location that looks like our fantasy. This location is a daily reality for someone or something. Until now, we have not built sets especially for a film. We'll change little things about a location, but not a lot. But we never make documentaries. We're traditional in that sense: for us, art is a depiction, a picture, or an image – and thus a mental construct. We also don't understand why nowadays there's so much discussion about art being artificial, because we thought art has always been artificial. We thought that's the essence of it. Art is artificial, and we like that.

We think it becomes a problem when artists pretend their art is reality, like all those photographers who make stylized "snapshots". This whole movement that investigates the borders between "fake" and "real" seems quite uninteresting and trivial to us. For us personally, there's never been a doubt about what's real and what's artificial. What's false will never be true, even if we don't know that it's false.

N. SCH.: Your works are also deeply romantic. They result from the exploration of the past. However, they don't show any way to make something out of the past, or divulge what might be. Is the utopian moment at all possible in the current art world?

D. RI./D. RO.: Not being able to think in utopian terms would be very grim indeed. We think art deals with sublime moments, dreams, fantasies, and prophesies. The more emotions you experience while watching an art piece, the better it is. We'd love to make a work that would make everyone cry.

But we're not sure if it's utopia we're dealing with. We see our pieces more as a visualization of an assumption of a certain reality. We want to make a film about everything. We don't know yet when we'll make it. Lately, we've been watching a lot of epic films: *Lawrence of Arabia*, *Barry Lyndon*. The epic is Hollywood's interpretation of everything.
We don't think it's possible to make art without believing in utopia. It wasn't in the past, and is still not, today. We think every artist has visions of sublime beauty. We all want to outdo ourselves, to make the ultimate piece, and we all work in order to be remembered after our deaths. We think artists who don't work in this frame of mind can only comment on their own identity crisis.

N. SCH.: You say – and show, too – that time is an essential, important part of your work. So why don't you then deal with the present?

D. RI./D. RO.: Yes, we think that looking at a beautiful image takes a certain amount of time. In a way, we're on a mission to preserve a number of beautiful images that we have in our heads. Images are being used as garbage. People don't even look at them.
That's why we're not so eager to make another image every week. People won't even notice, and besides, we don't work that fast. Probably no artist does.
It is also our task to protect the images we made from over-exposure, and our public from their self-imposed visual bulimia.

Last week, a graphic designer asked us to give him some images for an article in a Dutch art magazine. When we gave him three photos, he laughed in our faces and said, "Only three?" Then, while looking at each slide, holding it against the light on the ceiling for about two seconds, he said, "This isn't an image". Only one of the three photos passed as image for him. It's a slide of a sparsely clad young girl with big tits. Nu magazine's designers asked us for "ten images or more, so we can choose..." When we sent only two, to diminish the option of choice, they decided to use one of our illustrations as a background color for the (excellent) text. The thing is, we don't even have ten images lying around, because we're not image factories.

When we were young, there used to be one fashion magazine in Holland, called *Avenue*. *Avenue* emphasized its monopolistic position in the modern way: it preached the truth and nothing but the truth. If Wina Born (*Avenue's* culinary correspondent) opposed basil in her column, you wouldn't want to be caught dead putting basil anywhere because you'd be OUT. None of the solemn readers would have a single doubt about it. Wina Born's authority was unshakeable.
It was pure style dictatorship. Very modern, and so easy! No need to make a choice or take a position. This saved time and confusion. Maybe it's old-fashioned to believe in clarity, but we do.

In the mid-eighties, *Avenue's* reputation started to fade; other magazines emerged. The editors came up with a very post-modern idea: the *Avenue* Box. This box would have different ingredients each month, based on a different theme, i.e., the Japanese box that contained, among other items, two chopsticks... *Avenue* went bankrupt soon after. Their former chief editor now runs *APMagazine*, a free monthly published by a minor Dutch supermarket chain.

N. SCH.: You want your works to be regarded as images. You make films. Do you think of yourselves as filmmakers?

D. RI./D. RO.: We're artists, and we make films.

N. SCH.: In *Forever and Ever*, from 1995, you're most clearly operating with the theatricalism of the photo-novel. The camera work in the film gives more of a suggestion of film stills, very carefully arranged in a series. Haven't you misused the form here? Wouldn't the photo-novel have been enough? Wouldn't it have been the more appropriate medium? Isn't the form here just coquetry?

D. RI./D. RO.: No, *Forever and Ever* is more than a series of images. First of all, they are not still. Time moves in every image, and this can be felt. The underlying sounds and the timing create feelings of suspense, expectation, space, concentration. Editing feels like making music. It's like a composition.
We want to tell a story in every film we make. A narrative is formed by an image, combined with a sound and its duration. As soon as time passes, a story is told. Even if nothing moves in an image, a viewer will create his own narrative. Also, the presentation guides the expectation toward a narrative.
Anticipation forms the first part of the story. Even before the film starts, you know there will also be an end. So the story is in between.

N. SCH.: "Moving images" are hip. You've participated in numerous such genre exhibitions. However, since your installation instructions are intricate, this appears to me to be a contradiction. After all, don't you build environments or spaces, where the "moving image" is just a product of coincidence?

D. RI./D. RO.: We make our installations with a great deal of concentration. In an assigned or self-chosen space, we try to create an atmospheric mix between cinema and exhibition space. The films we make have a specific beginning and end, and should be watched in their entirety. Viewings take place, for instance, twice every hour. A timetable on the wall informs a viewer of the projection times. There are some benches for viewers to sit on. The space is clean, empty, and half-dark, so its dimensions are still perceptible. All disturbing elements, such as lights, reflections, or noises are reduced as much as possible. We take special care to provide for the peripheral vision of people sitting on the benches. The projector is placed in a soundproof box. This box, and all other elements placed in the room (speakers, benches) are purely functional. The way they are placed in the room is important, because during an exhibition the room is usually not filled with film. We perceive this room as a minimal sculpture.
So these spaces are more than rooms in which you experience things. They are developed especially for showing the films we make, and they're also supposed to function even when no film is projected in them. In our films, emptiness is as important as it is in the projection spaces we design.
We also figured out that the public is conditioned in all sorts of ways, and we try to create a situation where it is possible for an audience to concentrate on a film without being uncomfortable. The context in which a work is shown influences the piece and the viewers' reception of it, so we feel the work extends far beyond its frame. If we made paintings, we would do the same.

N. SCH.: You've often said that exhibitors primarily neglect sound, regarding it as unimportant. How do you explain this carelessness? Or is it actually that there are fundamental communication problems about the presentation of art between the artist and the exhibition location? Is that why you place so much value on strict adherence to your concept of how to stage your installations?

D. RI./D. RO.: In most group shows, sound producing artists like we are asked to let the soundtracks of their pieces be mixed with the others, to create one overall, random composition. This usually becomes clear about an hour before the opening, and the artists are expected to get together and "talk about it". The most humiliating thing is to have to negotiate with your fellow artist. You both know that, once again, a compromise will be shown.
Sufficient measures to avoid these painful moments and the needless amputation of the art pieces are usually not taken, due to money shortage, ignorance, or because "the continuity of the show" ought not to be disturbed. But what's the need for continuity in a show when only half of every piece can be experienced?

Most curatorial work seems to be done on the basis of image or content, sometimes even both. But if curators want to insist upon making their own compositions from the sounds of different pieces, maybe they should start by collecting the soundtracks.
It's crazy and lazy, of course, to think that one part of an art piece needs less attention then another. Or that one part is less important. It's like showing two sculptures on top of each other.
But a curator cannot be blamed for not knowing how to show an art piece. The artist should tell him/her. Some artists don't mind if the sound of their piece is mixed with others. Some even like it. But if all the ones who don't keep accepting insufficient conditions for showing their pieces, nothing will change.

N. SCH.: Then what is your attitude toward curatorial authorship?

D. RI./D. RO.: It seems strange that many of the star curators become famous for their group shows. It's precisely those group shows that are so problematic for artists. We don't make a piece thinking about how it could function in a group show.
Curatorial authorship might nowadays be a reason why so many artists extend their pieces into the entire exhibition space.
It's a reason why many of us need separate rooms or boxes or booths – as protection from curatorial horror.
Luckily, when a curatorial concept stinks, most intelligent people will just laugh about it and try to discover the art underneath the crap. But that doesn't make it right.

Some curators are very good, of course. They have an original vision. It was great to work with Harm Lux, for instance.
He can actually add something interesting to a piece, and he's very smart and committed.
Maybe the main problem with curatorial authorship is that, since it's been invented, we can't go back. We'll never be able to look at two art pieces again without thinking why they were put together, and by whom...
A new development in curatorial assertiveness is the desire to produce: more and more, you hear curators criticize their colleagues for organizing shows with pretentious themes and embarrassing titles. The new curator doesn't do all that, but can't wait to proudly say, "Oh, you know that piece by so-and-so? Yeah, I produced that..." The new curator says, "I produced that" or "I showed that piece first".
It means that curators developed within a short period of fifteen years, from bureaucratic organizers who operated in the shadows, to context makers (of thematic exhibitions), to inventors ("I discovered that piece practically before the artist did and showed

it an hour later"), to producers.

Of course it is great and very necessary nowadays for exhibition makers to be involved with more complicated, expensive, and time-consuming production processes. But when it becomes just another means of demonstrating their self-suspected generosity, an artist might prefer to have the ugly logo of some anonymous sponsor elaborately printed on their piece. False integrity doesn't add anything to a piece of art.

VEIT LOERS
OBSERVATIONS ON DE RIJKE/DE ROOIJ'S *OF THREE MEN*

The latest film by the artists Jeroen de Rijke and Willem de Rooij,
Of Three Men, is their most prodigious: 35 mm, 10 minutes long.
A comparatively elaborate format, a painstaking arrangement, and
a mise en scène of cinematic standards await the viewer in the
museum. One sees an empty, dark room, in which a wall is opened
to reveal the view of a church interior. A significant part of the work
consists of the staging – not just with regard to the screening requi-
rements, but also in light of the film's content. A view of a church
interior is staged, but there is no action on stage. The gaze does not
exactly meet a void, but the stationary position of the camera is the
allegorical location of a void. Perhaps it is also the relationship of the
viewer to the cinema. Or the prologue to the screening and the
darkened room – of significance here is what unwinds in the cinema,
in the literal sense of the word. But it is also more than that. The ten
minutes of film and the interior of an Amsterdam church projected
onto a wall are the essentials.

The film's production circumstances are not decisive, but they do
provide a starting point. The church is not a medieval building,
but was built in the early twenties – the latest historicism, already
part of modern architecture. A Gothicism of surfaces, lines, and
space. A feeling of weightlessness overwhelms one – a condition
that simultaneously conveys something of the cubist church paintings by Delaunay and Feininger. Another aspect is the emptiness of
the church. It was converted to a mosque and its entrance relocated
to the rear. Thus, it does without the pews that would otherwise
clutter up the nave. With its chandeliers, the house of God emerges
in the kind of purity that had once seduced the Romantics into
restoring Baroque-furnished Gothic cathedrals to their original state,
in order to regain a presumably lost fiction of space.

The size of the film's image and the nuances of color explain why
de Rijke/de Rooij used the medium of film, specifically 35 mm film.
Video installations today create effects through their large dimensions,
made possible by video projectors. Barnett Newman, Mark Rothko,

and Clifford Still's formats, the volume of the works by Donald Judd, Carl Andre, and Richard Serra, and the size of cibachromes made by photographers have, since the eighties, all been concerned with the proportions of the viewer in relation to the works.

One should at least have the desire to enter de Rijke/de Rooij's church interior. The degree of devotion increases; the gaze is not that of television's strained voyeuristic illusionism. It is not the illustration of another boundless world that focuses interest, but rather the gaze enters, relaxed, into a world of approximately the same size. This gives one the feeling of actually being in the space, although this is not possible, since the image is just a mirage, as is all film space. Yellow-ochre, as well as gray tones permeated with blue contrast determine the general color concept.

As we have said, the interior space consists of an unusual synthesis of the latest historicism and early Modern architecture. It is an interior that already seems to have been made for the film. The scenery corresponds to the medieval, painterly sets from films made by Fritz Lang (*Die Nibelungen*), Paul Wegener (*Golem*), and F. W. Murnau (*Faust, Nosferatu*) in the nineteen-twenties. The shape of the walls of the nave and aisles create a spatial image that is not only architecturally planned, but also underscored by the directors' slight shifting of the camera from its central axis. The wide-angle of the objective lens opens up the space and yet, at the same time, lends it a closeness that is needed to define a location. On the other hand, the absolute central perspective creates a forced spatial progression terminating in an imaginary vanishing point.

The paintings of church interiors by Pieter Saenredam (1597-1665) are significant for de Rijke/de Rooij's concept of the film.

The Haarlem painter was one of the most important masters of this genre, which one could most certainly call the church portrait. It has been discovered that Saenredam changed central perspective in accordance to the natural elements of the church. By slightly shifting the central perspective and lighting, he was able to create a new type of visionary space, whose lighting betrays that one is dealing with more than just a Protestant church interior freed from its Catholic altars. In the eighteenth century, the *scena per angolo* (i.e., the stage-set with two points of perspective) was used to rotate the space, so to speak, in order to shift a corner toward the viewer. This idea brought greater proximity and verisimilitude to viewers at a greater distance, experienced not just in Baroque sets, but also in the *Carceri* by Piranesi. The film *Of Three Men*, however, is shot from a nearly central perspective. With its wide-angle perspective and architectural concept (which should be regarded as an image), the viewer nevertheless experiences a fullness of space containing its own discrete scenery that is, at the same time, isolated.

Now there are moments that emerge from imagery to affect the film. In the first scene, several people with draperies function as a curtain, which then suddenly opens. The choreography is then elevated to a qualitatively higher plane. One cosmically experiences the standstill in the former church – like the exhalation of a Brahmin. The slowly rotating chandeliers activate the calm experienced. The sun and clouds outside cause a further sequence of movements, which vary the lighting in the church. Finally, one cannot overlook the nearly imperceptible movements of the people who keep the image in flowing motion. On the right, in the background behind the nave, three men sitting on the floor are visible, bowing up and down in prayer. A barely noticeable figure on the left, and another man, who later enters the scene from the right, are also parts of this living rhythm. The space breathes through these elements. Although hardly visible, these believers are the external and internal parameters for the inner grandeur and transcendence of the house of God.

Image, space, and temporal continuity also emerge, however, through the uncut, ten-minute shot, in which the aspect of sustained time becomes especially visible. The added soundtrack is a hard-to-define, permanent noise, a thematization of spatial calm, penetrating from outside and shrouding the scene like a veil. All of these moments in time, containing silence filled with sound, result in something quite odd. The revelation of space becomes permanent. Whereas at the beginning of the film, the dominant sensation was that one could lose oneself within the filmed space of the church – or, rather, mosque – this notion is quickly abandoned. The zoom does not open any wider. In terms of film technique, everything has been achieved, and the prospect of the church begins to assume temporal dimensions. It is like a kind of waiting, and the constant noise allows this waiting to be heard. It is only in a condition of relative boredom, or, more euphemistically stated, meditation, that one becomes aware of the three men as they emerge in half-shadows from the dusk. They are the measure of space, appearing as the source of its spatial-ethereal substance, although they are at once dissolved in it. In addition, the praying figures lend the space a historical dimension. In Islam, the prayer stance has remained archaic. One has the impression that one has ended up in some indescribable historical building. Saenredam and his contemporaries, like Hendrick van Steenwijk the younger, portray in their church interiors the sacrifice of Melchizedek or the nocturnal liberation of Peter. Nearly a century earlier, with his St. Florian Sebastian altar, Albrecht Altdorfer had already placed Pontius Pilate washing his hands in the context of a Gothic church and, with his famous birth of Mary, now in Munich's Alte Pinakothek, made a hall church the place of action.

De Rijke/de Rooij's films are concerned with what is timely, in the form of what is timelessly valid. The apparition of the butterfly and its symbolism of vanity; the endurance of love, even on a photograph; India today, subsumed in the Nirvana of the cosmos; the encounter with the iceberg, whose unapproachability and purity are of perceptible duration. From a proper distance, history and

geological history are shyly probed, in the search for ways to depict them. The camera, long since accustomed to immediate proximity and indiscretion, becomes an almost neutral picture-taking instrument not meant to move the images, bringing them closer; but rather to return to them their original dignity and distance. This is also a return to an audience that has largely forgotten how to perceive the dignified aspects of images, above all because the worldwide appropriation of images by the media has taken its toll. More than twenty years ago in Holland, Jan Bas Ader made similarly tranquil films *Farewell to Faraday Friends* (1971) or *Flower Works* (1974) with long shots; they were, however, less epic than mildly ironic. Other pieces from the seventies belonging to this category are unquestionably Marcel Broodthaers' cinematic work and that of his friend David Lamelas. But even the cinema has left its traces in the still recent oeuvre of de Rijke/de Rooij. For example, Stanley Kubrick allows interior space to speak or remain silent in his films, as if it were an independent entity – i.e., in his spaces, one sees fewer sequences than images.

Minimal Art was not only the form of a new spatial constructivism; it was even more the expression of a new statement about space. The absolute, which we are more likely to conceive of as anorganic, became connected with space – or to put it more precisely, with cubical space. Minimal Art flourishes in the aquarium-like space of the art museum. De Rijke/de Rooij's films similarly demand a cubical space in order to appear in their optimal form. These cubes must be dark so that the laws of film can take effect. The exhibition space, which nowadays peacefully coexists with Minimal Art, inverts its function and becomes, in its emptiness and darkness, the ideal place for the appearance of purified film images.

De Rijke/de Rooij do not only associate historical fantasies with the filmed present and the transformation of what is Christian into what is Islamic, but evoke the ancient unity of the three monotheistic religions: Judaism, Christianity, and Islam. Rembrandt – who delved into the world of the Old Testament, in which bearded figures upon occasion decorously act like dervishes – was not only motivated by his commissions. The present moment is perceptible in the ascetic parables – a synthesis of spirituality, whose rapture will never become a historical image. Helena Blavatskij's theosophical movement at the end of the nineteenth century, which attempted a synthesis of the important world religions, was of enormous significance in Amsterdam at the beginning of the modern age, and had numerous followers, particularly among artists. The clarity of Protestantism once again received a new set of wings. Perhaps this historical-temporal background is like an art-historical parable: Modern art (especially Abstract and Minimal Art), anchored in Western history, found in Islam – particularly in Sufism – a symbol for its inherent iconoclasm. The Sufi must learn to bring the world of thought, the world of feeling, and the physical world into equilibrium. Time is an attribute of God. In *Of Three Men*, the uneventful church space does not want to be seen, but rather experienced. The Sufi attempts to blend the unity of the external image with what is inside himself. What is outside of the self is actually within. When de Rijke/de Rooij's film is over, the image burns on within. Perhaps one can also describe this feeling with Francis de Assisi's saying: "What you are searching for is that which searches".

VANESSA JOAN MÜLLER
NON-FICTION

The film works of Jeroen de Rijke and Willem de Rooij are cinema in its decontextualized form. These films operate within the dispositive structure of the medium and its conventions: projection in a darkened space, a precisely defined beginning and ending, and the latent obligation to watch the film in its entirety. However, de Rijke/ de Rooij situate themselves and their films in the framework of institutionalized art; they position their projectors in the familiar ambiance of the art museum's "white cube". Admission is paid at the museum's cashier.

This advanced de- and re-contextualization affects not only the framework of what one could call the mechanical appearance of the film image, but also the framework of the film images themselves, whose references can be found in visual art as well as in cinema – though primarily in art. The coordinates of this aesthetic reference system have shifted with time, from Minimalist Abstraction to Abstract Expressionism, and then three hundred years back to the Dutch Baroque. There is nevertheless a constant in the films of de Rijke/de Rooij that unites this aesthetic divergence, providing their entire work with a linear structure. Besides the reductionist element that subjects the categories of angle, edit, and camera movement to their essential minimum, there is also the aspect of prolonged time. In the work of de Rijke/de Rooij, the classic time-space continuum – in which space is crossed and time flows – is nearly transformed to movement in standstill. To use Gilles Deleuze's substantial cinematographic classification, the artists' films can be said to deliver not "images of movement"[01], but instead moving images that separate the visible from things, and movement from history, favoring time as a category of aesthetic experience. Here, time in film means the sculpting of the fixed, perceptible, apparently decelerated yet real presence of the projected image in its sensory appearance.

01 VGL. GILLES DELEUZE, *DAS BEWEGUNGS-BILD. KINO 1*. FRANKFURT/M. 1989.

As the temporalization of perception, time – simultaneously perceiving and perceptible – makes human perception temporal, directing the gaze to various reference systems, the inner framework and order of visibility. Defining the visible, these systems reintegrate the medium of film into the classic system of image production by subjecting the norms and aesthetics of the static image to a transfer through media. To locate the medium of film thus in an open referential system of existing visual parameters does not, however, mean to take iterative recourse to something existing. In de Rijke/de Rooij's films, the constructive rejection of linear narrative structures leads far more to an examination of the visual as a semiotically codified and aesthetic text that can always be read anew.

Chun Tian ("Spring", 1994) is the first joint film by Jeroen de Rijke/ Willem de Rooij; it exposes their overall aesthetic interest in liberating the structures of film. How much can one omit while still maintaining a circumscribed totality? How much distance to reality can the gaze tolerate? Which form of reduction constructs images of abstract beauty? The answer could be that, ultimately, it is precisely the purification of the narrative and the termination of the recognizably subjective signature of the auteur that constitute a film. With its constructive character, this film would combine the principle of beauty with a feeling of alienation that turns the gaze even more forcefully to the beauty of its images.

Chun Tian stages the exotic as a minimalist postcard-impression that could be shot everywhere and nowhere. In fact, the exotic scene takes place in the Amsterdam botanical gardens, although it appears in the image as a difficult-to-place construct beyond cultural specificity. Sensual magnolia blossoms, filling the screen, are the first thing that one sees – almost a cliché, but also a setting that the image seems to transform into a photograph, repeated at the speed of twenty-four images per second. Then the camera tracks slowly to the left, and an Asian couple appears standing completely motionless in the midst of the glorious blossoms: a tableau vivant of geometrical abstraction. On the right, the woman gazes at the man, but he looks past her and directly out of the image of the film. After the camera has rested on the two of them for a while, a subtitle appears ("You are really very beautiful"), but no one says anything. A moment later the sentence is heard in Chinese, from off-camera. It is a masculine voice, but whether it really belongs to the man on the screen remains as unclear as the language remains foreign. There follows a cut, and the geometric composition of the figure is presented in axial mirroring: now it is the man, who gazes at the woman while she looks to the left outside of the image. After a while, a voice is heard from off-camera, this time a feminine one. In this case, it is the subtitle ("I love you") which is seen only after a delay. The camera slowly zooms back until the couple is completely framed by the scenery of flowers. This would actually be a beautiful concluding image, coded as if it could remain forever so. Yet the film ends abruptly before one expects the ending; it undermines the fulfillment of its internal logic and ruins what the final image suggests. The suddenness of this rupture lets the feeling of beautiful appearance simply fall into nothingness and leaves a strange emptiness as a cutting-off from the thread of illusion.

Yet, what is also presented in *Chun Tian*, like a love story reduced to its basic parameters, appears – in spite of the immediate beauty of the images – as an expression of the greatest dissociation; the story of declared affection, shortened to fragments, is staged as a series of abstract figurations within a standardized topos. In this way, the classic I-love-you, actually presupposing a subject and an object as well as an affective link between the two, appears to be reduced to its lexical dimension. Here, love is in fact only a word. By differentiating the linguistic and the visual, and with its deictic ruptures, *Chun Tian* has a certain quality regarding the filmic and semantic decomposition that shifts the whole into something like an abstract experimental procedure. Instead of a narrative, only formal closure visibly inscribes structure into the image. Left and right, writing and voice, inside and outside: these dichotomies are the actual organizational factors alongside the intensity of the colors and the suggestive aesthetic of the composition.

Thus, the frame determining the composition remains indirectly visible, precisely because the internal pictorial structure of the gaze damages it so vehemently. The gaze to the outside of the frame demands in itself an ensuing shot that shows the object of the gaze so that spatiotemporal coherence is maintained. In de Rijke/de Rooij's work, on the contrary, the camera remains focused the entire time on the figures while it slowly moves intermittently to the left along a strictly horizontal plane. Nothing exists outside of the currently visible, not even virtually. Additionally, the movement from right to left contradicts the conventions of filmic representation, for the images of film are also typically read from left to right. Thus, from the very beginning, the gaze stumbles in the wrong direction. Moreover, it is only the camera that moves in this continuous place of action, whereas the figures stand there as if frozen solid. The result is the impression of a discontinuous movement that functions like a succession of still images, although the film only consists of two long shots. In contrast to montage, which switches the image, this slow movement only alters it and lets the scene glide along the camera like a colorful panorama.

However, *Chun Tian* is not only concerned with the de-fictionalization of illusion by contravening the conditions of flowing movement. The subtitles, mechanically imprinted on the celluloid, do much more to accentuate the two-dimensionality of the filmic image by lying on the surface like a membrane and marking what is behind them as an artificial representation. The only cut is the classic match cut, the dialectical cut connecting two different scenes by repeating or duplicating the plot and the form. It presents two variants of the same thing, thus directing the gaze to the formal correspondences as well as differences that constitute this reversed relationship. For example, the fundamental dichotomy of voice and writing, presence and representation is pushed to the frontiers of the film and thereby put out of commission. As a material marking, writing stands for the outside, for the belated addition of the translation. It is figured as a substitutive *supplement* [02] for the absent voice, while the voice serves as an indicator of corporeal presence. However, the writing of the subtitles as well as the voice are external additions to *Chun Tian*. Even the voice is outside of the image, and is a belated addition, a supplement to the writing. Off camera, it is outside of the image and of time. It does not belong to a person who is present but is instead bound to the text. There is also the transfer from one language to the other, revising the hierarchical structure of the before and after. The subtitle translates what is being said. In the second variation, when the voice first comes in after the subtitle, it is the voice that figures as a translation of writing. Thus the one completes the other, and both voice and writing appear as signs attempting to fill up an absence. Yet their function is not substitutive but rather purely additive. In any case, they remain remarkably alien to the image as bearer of sense and meaning. Because the people are also only building blocks within the symmetrical field of the image, selected coordinates and directional vectors of a perfect composition inscribed within the frame, the viewer doesn't really care who is actually speaking.

02 JAQUES DERRIDA: *GRAMMATOLOGIE*, FRANKFURT/M. 1974. S. 250 F.

FOREVER AND A DAY

Compared to the painterly abstraction of the above, de Rijke/
de Rooij's next work almost develops the qualities of a feature film.
Forever and Ever (1995) is a film about film, just as *I'm Coming
Home in Forty Days*, two years later, will be a film about painting:
unknown but somehow also familiar images, nevertheless not direct
citations, that have the effect of aesthetically alienating what is
known. The referents are less from painting than from cinema.
However, cinema's historically and culturally coded ways of seeing
are not as easily escapable, for the question of the story told by a
film is also a question of the rules to which it submits. Therefore,
the deconstruction of the images and the structures organizing them
is formulated as close as possible to these images and structures,
the building blocks of the genre, its mannerisms and established
codes. As a challenge to the legacy of Hollywood, the soap opera,
and the Indian cinema of great gestures and feelings, *Forever and
Ever* is also a film about the permanent hesitation that indicates
without drawing consequences; it tells fragments of a story that
does not exist at all. Although it recognizes the form of narrative
as a play of difference, it depicts it only as an empty contour.
By dividing the filmic grammar and liberating its conventional elements, de Rijke/de Rooij strip the matrix of film's history down
to its bare bones; what structure remains is a visual remix of what
can be told in the in-between of the shots, while still retaining the
idea that something can in fact be told. This renders especially difficult the retranslation of the images into language, which is always a
problem, for there is no narrative pattern onto which the description
could fall back. "Plot" proves to be more of a by-product of the
additive ordering of images. The narrative order becomes a product
of the existing gaps that constitute the surface plot precisely in their
function as absence. In the end, film therefore presents shards of
a cinematic aesthetic that constructs its variation of what is always
the same with the abstraction of images and of filmic grammar.
Forever and Ever operates within the factors of frame, time, and space

41

in such a way that the visible is not treated as an excerpt but rather as the setting and fragment of a virtual totality. The framing of images brings out a frontality without background that emphasizes the film as film: a two-dimensional sign-system that points to a pictorial and referential relation to reality. This sign-system is fundamentally oriented, however, to the physical presence of the viewer, who recognizes the "outside" of the image solely as an imaginary museum from film and television.

The first camera movement also circumscribes a topography of seeing, whenever it constructs a space in which the scene of the presentation is anchored for the gaze at the scene. Here, the first space stands completely under the sign of painting, when *Forever and Ever* begins with a slow pan across an Indian bay with the beautiful name "The Queen's Necklace", with the horizon exactly in the center of the image. The sky and the sea are two almost monochromatic abstract layers of blue; the dominant color remains blue even as the city skyline moves into the image. Due to the widely opened exposure, the panorama depicted by the slow pan loses all depth and horizon. When a woman's face appears in close-up in the ensuing shot, the contrast could hardly be any greater. This woman in front of the bay is a classic portrait with plastically modeled foreground and shimmering background. A clear differentiation of sharpness within the image is dominant in painting; this sharpness extends along parallel and successive layers of the image, each of which is autonomous and determined by adjacent elements. Every layer of the image, above all the entire foreground, has its own theme and its own value in the overall theme, and yet they all come together to form a unity. Structurally, the landscape and the face therefore constitute a correlation in which the landscape is placed according to the face and the one is treated like the other. Even the close-up in film elevates the face to a landscape modulated by light and shadow. The face is the pure raw material of the affect, a re-coded surface separated from the body and deterritorialized from the head.[03] However, the affect produced by the woman's face here is nothing more than the knowledge of being observed, of having completely become an image. She stands on the balcony of one of the houses on the bay framed by the vertical lines of the balcony; this is an architectonic pattern, a framing within the image, that creates new aesthetic delineations. First, she gazes directly at the viewer, but then to the right outside of the image: frontal view, half-profile, profile. The bay appears to be transformed in the hazy background, and even the sound, clearly present in the beginning, is reduced to a subtle background noise. Spatial depth is only created by overlapping various spatial layers; in its composition, the image itself is presented as a two-dimensional tableau.

This beginning is actually a classic establishing shot setting the stage for what will happen, yet introducing the protagonist with an insistence on pictoriality that lends everything an iconic quality not connected with any narrative structure. Nevertheless, the usual parameters of conventional cinema all appear at some point: the landscape as the metaphoric space of the city-person's flight, the walk along a lake, the investigative tour through a deserted villa, and finally the great romantic finale in the starry night. And precisely these cinematographic codes and conventions give the images a semiotic and aesthetic charge that binds them, in the end, to an imaginary unity. Therefore, images which are almost static can depict nothing more than the things themselves, while a series of landscape panoramas in slow motion is replaced by a series of deserted interiors which formulate the idea of a villa more than they depict one concretely. The demontage of the illusion immanent to film succeeds precisely by dividing the coherence of the filmic whole

03 SEE GILLES DELEUZE AND FÉLIX GUATTARI, "DAS JAHR NULL – GESCHICHTLICHKEIT" IN: VOLKER BOHN, ED. *BILDLICHKEIT* (FRANKFURT/M., 1990) 438F. SEE ALSO GILLES DELEUZE, *CINEMA* 1. *THE MOVEMENT-IMAGE* (MINNEAPOLIS: U. OF MINNESOTA PRESS, 1983).

into separate unities. As a film, *Forever and Ever* is organized into more or less equally long sequences separated by black screens and constituting abstract blocks, blocks that replicate the course of the day: the bay in the morning, the sea, the house, the sky at night. India, where the film was shot, is near and far at the same time, just as the landscape pictures of early travelers always include referential frames of their homelands in their impressions of faraway places. In light of our global culture, this is hardly necessary if one does not want to decidedly elevate the alterity of the Other to a subject. The ubiquity of remarkably extraterritorial non-places bears nothing of the European's anthropological interest in the exotic. Instead, a distanced gaze is directed to abstract panoramas of landscape and architecture, at once real and foreign. Now the same somehow always appears in the different, and on the other hand, even the particular in the general. This does not mean a formalist recourse to a structural universe that transforms all places into a nowhere. Instead, the rejection of cultural difference and specificity itself reproduces the structures of the alluded genres of film, which are determined by a capitalist logic of globalization.

The structures' classic determinants of plot and characters, in which space is to be crossed and time is flowing, are consequently ruined by the structure of distantly reflected observation. In de Rijke/de Rooij's films, the people simply run to the camera and then out of the picture. People converse, but it never becomes clear what their talk is really about, and the people in the picture themselves remain mute. It seems irritating that the privileged form of communication is the off-camera voice, while a visible relation between the picture and the voice never comes to be. Precisely because they are not diegetic – they apparently are not part of the plot – the voices are able to connect the shots without being subordinated to a narrative logic. Whenever someone leaves the visible space to the sides in the direction of the visually negated space beyond the frame, he or she remains disappeared in *Forever and Ever*. Cinema formally insists that the field of the visible also possess an outside, a virtual space beyond the currently visible. Only the continuity of fiction – as logic of narration and possible sequence of events – defines in narrative cinema the place of the viewer as the place of the action. De Rijke/de Rooij, on the contrary, hold the viewer at a distance whenever they have the narrative take place solely in the empty space between the images. There is no separate here and there but instead only the actuality of what is currently visible.

Outdoor shots have the effect of large-format photography with cinematic presence. They bear in the minimal succession of camera movement the aura of painted panels capable of lengthy contemplation. In their two-dimensional composition, nature approaches the panoramic. As film images, they are purely iconic – at once semioticized landscape-space and stereotypical "sites". However, not only does the landscape appear epic, but the people in *Forever and Ever* are also filmed like things, with the same calmly observing distance that indicates how the gaze becomes slowly familiar with what it sees. As was already the case in *Chun Tian*, beauty is the topic, not only the beauty of the woman, but also that of the image. In *Forever and Ever* it is a couple who stands at the banks of a lake while the water frames them both as an ornamental structure: "It's beautiful, isn't it?" – "Yes, it's very beautiful". Not only is the lake beautiful, but also the image of the people in front of the lake; the commentary is a commentary from off-camera that could be a dialogue between the two people, but it could also be a dialogue *about the* two of them as a filmic composition.⁰⁴ In this way, the film-text and the meta-text are always shifted – gaze in the image and gaze

04 THE SCENE AT THE LAKE HAPPENS TO BE A CITATION FROM PETER YATES' FILM *BULLITT* (USA, 1968). THERE, IT HAS LESS TO DO WITH BEAUTY THAN WITH DISILLUSIONMENT IN THE FACE OF THE VIOLENCE TO WHICH THE PROTAGONIST, AS A POLICEMAN, IS SUBJECTED. THE CONTRAST – BETWEEN THE IMAGE AND THE TEXT – STRUCTURES THE IMAGE.

onto the image as an abstract tableau. But the end is near whenever the viewers begin to lose themselves in beauty. A sudden cut, and then the camera is already directed at a new place of action which will never occur – the interior in its alienated everyday quality.

The architectural inventory begins with a classic external shot from the garden; then a space with sofas can be seen in strictly centrally perspectival single shots, followed by the dining room, the fireplace room, and a gaze through glass doors back to the garden. Fragments of the space are presented in various shots without giving the impression, however, of a homogeneous situation. Whatever is presented in long, unmoving shots like rooms arranged one after the other, is put together into a single interior by the ensuing slow pan; the dining-room table is next to the terrace window, next to which the sofas and the fireplace can be seen. Everything seems abandoned, uninhabited, and the ringing of the telephone, which accompanies the entire sequence, is never answered. Daily life seems to play no role in this room. However, the camera, always operating in the descriptive mode, explores farther and discovers a stairway leading to the next floor. A pan through the bedroom in fact fixates on traces of presence – an obviously used bed, articles of clothing strewn about. And – the telephone stops ringing. What is still missing during the tour of the villa dissected into static fragments is the swimming pool on the rooftop terrace. Here one also finds presumably indications of presence. But the telephone starts to ring again, and everything is exactly as uncertain as it was before. Thus, tension repeatedly flees into emptiness for the sake of images that promise everything but give nothing because they are only images without conclusive evidence.

What the second gaze presents is the re/vision of one image by the other; it invites a sequence with what follows and a questioning of the norms and the obviousness of the genre itself. The images create the illusion of linear coherence if one associates them with narrative film and begins to read the shots as a series of interconnected events.

Still, the whole is also more than the sum of its parts if the interior, fragmented in single tableaus, suggests an architectonic dimension that is, as a product of serial addition, necessarily dissolved in the totalizing pan. As a realistic scene, this space is indeed defined by its parts; the joining of which is determined from the very beginning by filmic conventions that could nonetheless occur in many different ways. In the end it remains a formless entity that eliminates everything that happens or could happen in it for the sake of the pure potential of emptiness.[05]

The final sequence of *Forever and Ever* is therefore constructed as an absolute opposite of this spatial and affective uncertainty – exterior rather than interior space, nature instead of culture, people instead of emptiness, voices instead of noises. In art's system of reference, this means a return to the metaphysics of romanticism, to the chiaroscuro of landscape painting, to the dramatic staging of darkness and light. The degree of the color and light's intensity absorbs all concretely contoured form, and the landscape is transformed into the infinite expanse of space. Only the light of the campfire illuminates the faces of the actors and renders precise the contours of two boys observing the stars against the dark background of the night in an extremely contrasted effect. In *Forever and Ever* this play of the light of the campfire is upliftingly beautiful and full of metaphysical kitsch, a precisely planned romanticism from the heart of the illusion-machine, cinema. Light, darkness, and the infinite expanse of the firmament and stars: "Every star may be a sun to someone".

05 THEREIN RESTS THE ACTUAL AFFINITY NOT ONLY TO THE STEREOTYPICAL SPATIAL SCENERY OF THE SOAP OPERA, BUT ALSO OF THE SPECIFIC OCCUPATION OF SPACES IN MICHELANGELO ANTONIONI'S FILMS; HE DERIVES HIS GREATEST RESONATING EFFECTS FROM THE JUXTAPOSITION OF POPULATED AND EMPTY SPACE. BY UTILIZING COLOR WHICH ABSORBS EVERYTHING, ANTONIONI ELEVATES SPACE TO A POTENCY OF EMPTINESS, ACCORDING TO WHICH THE ACTION IS REALIZED AND COMES TO A CLOSE. THE AFFECTIVE AGENCY IS ONLY THAT OF SPACE LIBERATED FROM ITS COORDINATES; THIS SPACE IS DRIVEN TO COMPLETE EMPTINESS AND TO NEARLY UN-FIGURATIVE ABSTRACTION. SEE DELEUZE, *THE MOVEMENT-IMAGE*.

After the objects shown in the film have exchanged their visibility for their meaning and their presence for the story's dynamic, de Rijke/ de Rooij transform the images back into the raw matter of imagination. The concrete level of signs is shifted into the imaginary and then back again. The line distinguishing film from reality thus rests in the optional occupation of the gaze, which could also always be a different one. Similarly, the sounds are no longer functionally dependent but have instead declared their own function. The telephone, which one never gets to see, serves only the purpose of indicating with its absence the very category of absence; as an acoustic signal, it resonates through the empty space of its missing pictorial presence. However, this emptiness is not only emptiness as absence, but also a scenery-like emptiness which, as a lack of fixed meaning, only waits for fiction to take possession of it. The absence of what is lacking can be practically seen as a quality of the present. Within this imaginary presence of the fictive, the actual *difference* is articulated as *différance*, as a shifting postponement of sense and meaning and an indecisive alternation of the perspectives of structure and event. Contexts are not completely eliminated but are minimized. The bay is a promise and the landscape is the setting for a mystery; the house offers diffuse suspense, and the campfire romanticism becomes a clichéd intimacy in Technicolor. The genre sets the standard; the rest are images and their polysemy. Only the overlapping layers of coincidence and meaning constitutes sense. In the end, however, this fixation on the ordering patterns of space and time is also a form of appropriating reality that approaches a loss of reality. Hence the uncertain feeling of melancholia, of the loss (of sense?), in the abstraction of everything unequivocal in the world of unstable signs.

After this treatment of the syntagmatics of the filmic in its conventional form, in which content and emotion are constituted from standardized topoi and codes, *Voor Bas Oudt* (1996) shifts the parameters a little more in the direction of sensuality and semantics. *Voor Bas Oudt* [06] departs from the discursive space of possibilities and multiplications with its virtual horizon of constantly withdrawing meaning. A turn, if not a course correction, is marked, which reduces the tested parameters even further and lets narrative traces be absorbed into the pure presence of the image. The fact that the film consists only of one planned sequence and proceeds without edits is also a function of its length of one minute. Here, the assault on reality is also less deconstructive than phenomenological; the camera serves only the registration of external structures and surfaces.

At the beginning of *Voor Bas Oudt* there is an abstract geometrical structure of fan-shaped ordered lines moving concentrically toward the outside as ornamental configurations at the limit of the nonfigurative. The intense green color absorbs the object. In the structure's circumferences it becomes recognizable that it is the foliage of a tropical plant. The camera feels its way along the surface and focuses on a leaf on which a white butterfly is sitting. The moth flutters its wings lightly, holds them trembling for a moment, and then slowly closes them.

The film was shot with a boroscope, usually used for scientific recordings because of its extreme depth of field. With this camera, all layers of space can be reproduced without distortion, even in extreme close-ups. Because of the regulated sharpness of the surfaces, all of the elements develop into an equally viewable event. First, the structures within the image catch the eye: the pattern on the butterfly's wings with its network of black lines, the structure and materiality of the plastic foliage, and the tender fragility of the insect. *Voor Bas Oudt* appears to be a snapshot, a short study on rendering visual qualities visible; nevertheless, it does not fulfill any criterion of scientific documentation. It experiences a connotative charge

06   THE TITLE IS A DEDICATION TO ONE OF DE RIJKE / DE ROOIJ'S TEACHERS FROM THE

RIETVELD-ACADEMY IN AMSTERDAM.

obtainable only by film precisely by concentrating on the one image of the butterfly. In the slow observation there develops an entire poetic semiology of materials and bodies, of ornaments, colors, and textures.

As was already the case in *Chun Tian*, this short film also ends unexpectedly and apparently too soon; the gaze has barely been directed to the butterfly when the blackness of the film reel sublates the referential illusion of reality and transforms the image into a mere memory. *Voor Bas Oudt* only recognizes the incomplete moment as a point of fulfillment in time, as an empty point in time within a linear structure. The existential, metaphysical moment as the plot's finality plays no role here. There is only the abrupt rupture in filmic time, which can only be continued in the imaginary. This calculated cut with the reality of illusion – stopping when it is at its most beautiful – creates a reference to the symbolic system of iconography, to which the image of the butterfly takes recourse. Like in the mimesis of painting, the things are as they are, and yet they are also something more. Butterflies inhabit the still lifes of the Dutch Baroque, for they are the perfect sensual image of *vanitas*, of the transitoriness of all earthly things. The butterfly is reminiscent of the impossibility of eternity and of eternal entropy. It celebrates the transitory moment and also reflects in this transitoriness the passing time documented by the shortness of the film. A moment of beauty after the metamorphosis (the butterfly has just crawled out of its cocoon) then this moment has already passed by.

Metaphorically, the butterfly symbolizes the three ontological manifestations of time – Being, Becoming, and Presence – in their materialization as Form, Appearance, and Existence.[07] The process of transition – because nothing else so eloquently bespeaks it from the iconography of *vanitas* – is therefore also a variant of the topos of time presented in its tragic finality. Just as *vanitas* sublimates its

07 SEE ONFRAY, *DIE FORMEN DER ZEIT. THEORIE DES SAUTERNES* (BERLIN, 1999) 120.

message of the metaphysics of death in images of discrete beauty, this butterfly, in its tropical microcosm, is also present in the affirmative beauty of the time of the now.

REALISTIC ABSTRACTION

Words serve to name things while, at the same time, things constitute themselves through language – no signifier without signified.
Language is not to be understood here as the replication of an already
present object that finds its designation within language. It is once
something has been named, communicated, that this something
first acquires the discursive form necessary for it to be exchanged
as a sign. The case is similar for space since the boundaries of
spatial reality are established through perception. It is in reference
to other things, particularly to those of individual experience, that
space is formed, that it takes shape. A favorite example used by
linguists to demonstrate the degree to which specific cultural
perception is inscribed in the structuring of language is that of the
Eskimos, whose language has nearly twenty different words for
snow. Since this element forms such a central category for the
inhabitants of the northern polar region, they name it precisely in
its many diversifications. The Inuit people possess a linguistic
phenomenology of snow that is completely foreign to European
understanding, since our language reduces to a summary concept
a perceptual image that has only been weakly conceived.
Thus the real and its images provoke concepts, and concepts,
in turn, provoke images. Beyond the dichotomies of reality and
subjectivity, appearance and meaning, signifier and signified, film –
or, more precisely, the cinematographic image – is apparently in the
position to produce a particular order within the visual field, in which
the image can be opposed to the concept.[08] For it is only in the
image that the legibility of the sign is immediately bound to its pure
visibility. What happens in film on the level of the visible is the result
of a structured assault on the real, insofar as film provides things
with a visuality not only grounded in the substantive absence of these
things and the resulting representative difference, but also constitutes

08 SEE MICHAEL KÖTZ, *DER TRAUM, DIE SEHNSUCHT UND DAS KINO. FILM UND DIE WIRKLICHKEIT DES
IMAGINÄREN* (FRANKFURT/M. 1986), 83.

– as the double of the real – a continual postponement. Therein lies the fundamental difference in the construction of "real" versus filmic reality, world-images versus image-worlds, with respect to their effects and their reconfiguration of what is real.

I'm Coming Home In Forty Days (1997), produced during a four-week trip to Disko Bay in Greenland, is a film dealing with time and the perception of time, where the iceberg, the subject of the film, stands for a piece of frozen past. The shimmering ice represents, in its very existence, the constant transition of the current concept of time. Here, however, the category of time also deals immediately with the cognitive appropriation of things, the manner in which we grasp things and fix them mnemotechnically, since time and memory are on parallel tracks. This depiction through media attempts to undermine the irretrievability of what has been seen, which can occasionally be remembered later in its continuous quality. In this respect, *I'm Coming Home in Forty Days* is also concerned with sounding out the boundary of re/presentation understood as the re-presencing of something past, with the structural similarity of image and memory, riddled with projections, and therefore never a wholly realistic replication and imagination.

In documentary form, film formulates a predetermination for condensed meaning insofar as it elevates that which one already expected to the level of certainty within the medium of the moving image. Film operates within predefined views, codes, and semiotizations and derives its legitimacy from these. *I'm Coming Home In Forty Days*, on the other hand, poses a much more abstract question: to produce the same condensed meaning with something previously unknown; that is, to bring what has not yet been recognized into recognition without reducing seeing to the act of re-recognition. The iceberg is reconstructed first in the replication and then again in the perception of this replication. Thus it is also possible in this case to reconstruct reality, after the fact, by means of the replica, such that a difference between what is real and what is representation is always maintained. This difference would be the result not only of alienation via media but also of the ever-changing certainty of experience. Formally, this film consists of nothing more than three shots of varying lengths, in which a ship slowly circles an iceberg. Hence the film carries the structure of a triptych which unfolds in succession by means of both spatial and temporal references and shifts. Whereas the classical triptych presents the construction of a temporal order by placing the Before and After in the side panels and the Now in the center panel, and thus presents a turning of the present moment towards its chronological frame of past and future, the film, into which the temporal moment is already inscribed, transfers this concept into the spatial dimension. In *I'm Coming Home In Forty Days*, it is the interference of different perspectives that represents disparate fields of perception of the same thing. This indicates less a play on reference – understood as a playing through of the possibilities both of seeing and of images – than an attempt to enclose the object within aesthetic experience. The visual totality first emerges out of a playing together of singularities that stage the Now of perception in relation to the past and future as the expression of a space-time continuum.

The film was shot under a misty early morning sky. Again and again the stereometric forms of the iceberg dissolve, change their appearance in the changing light perspective and melt into the gray-white sky. In this space composed of diffused light, which is difficult to localize, all solid substance bleeds into a transitory crossing over of matter and atmosphere. Only the opposition between water and iceberg maintains its clear contours. The film was shot in the fall, when the waters begin to thicken into ice. Hence the waves produced by the movement of the ship appear sluggish; the whole atmosphere implies a compromise or coming together of the individual elements. Since the point of view is that of the camera and is constantly shifting with the rocking of the ship, a vertiginous feeling is produced as the eye passes over the landscape. When the observed object cannot be precisely localized and the gaze gets lost in a nowhere between sky, ice, and wavering horizon, it is as if one had lost one's equilibrium.

The film was shot with a steadily adjusted, unwavering camera, with the focal length of the objective lens focused on the iceberg in accordance with the specifications of the technical controls, leaving horizontal and vertical movement to be determined by the motion of the ship. While observing these images, the act of seeing continually congeals into pure substrate, and what it perceives appears to belong to a different order of the visible.

Filmic visibility differs radically from visibility in the real since its essence lies within the discursive space of signs. These signs make present what is absent insofar as the visibility of the object is severed from its material presence and is subordinated to an isolated re/pre-sentation. Film takes place where the real is absent. In any case, the phenomenology of the filmic image, as pure visibility, dematerializes prior visibility. Yet whereas the former is referentially bound to the latter, it does not refer directly to the presence of any entity. This is due to the fact that direct visibility of the object is bound to a world of appearance in which visuality is always only the external visibility of the surface. Completion of perception by means of the other senses takes place outside the image; in the image, object and visibility are identical since the object of the image is itself merely surface.

In this way, the image constitutes its own reality by absolutizing the visible into matter without substance.[09] In *I'm Coming Home in Forty Days* fundamental phenomenologies such as these play a significant role.

Conceptually, film makes use of the irrevocable difference between seeing and knowing, namely the contradiction between what we

09 SEE LAMBERT WIESING, *DIE SICHTBARKEIT DES BILDES. GESCHICHTE UND PERSPEKTIVEN FORMALER ÄSTHETIK* (REINBEK BEI HAMBURG, 1997) 160.

know about the object presented and what can in fact be seen. Indeed, the filmic image of the iceberg does not correspond to the idea that the abstract concept "iceberg" evokes: the image shows neither a sheer, fissured surface, nor does it present the appearance of some thing jutting out of the water. On the contrary, the iceberg is characterized by its smooth rounded forms and has the effect of a compact dune in a desert of ice whose texture is more reminiscent of soft ice cream than firm, frozen matter. On the slow trip around the iceberg, it becomes clear that the iceberg possesses two very different faces; a smooth front and a split-open back, a concave and a convex arch. It is difficult to estimate its actual size; your sense of proportion and dimensionality disappears, since even the real surroundings appear abstract and indistinguishable. Hence, there is no recognition, in the sense of a rediscovery that merely reproduces familiar cultural knowledge.

Leading up to the travel project to Greenland and its resulting iceberg triptych was an initial series of photographs depicting icebergs of the polar region in their cool and distanced radiance. As photographs these icebergs evoke their own, alien atmosphere and appear as sculptural manifestations of a frozen past. They radiate an immediacy of presence, while at once producing a strange unreal effect, since icebergs are not exactly among the everyday objects appearing in our sphere of vision. As images, they radiate a familiarity that phenomenologically they do not in the least possess. Jeroen de Rijke/ Willem de Rooij, however, were interested in precisely this moment, in which the image and the real no longer relate to one another merely referentially but rather appear to be transported into a new relationship to one another by means of immediate experience. What is indirectly known beforehand through photographs places itself like an invisible membrane over the experience of the object during actual perception and thereby produces an irrevocable distance to what is perceived. This distance results from the comparison of what is known from reproduction with its actual referent. The visual facts of the Greenland icebergs immediately appear as a repetition of its photographic replica, since no optical reference is made available, no comparative moment of visual experience. External reality is grasped primarily through the optical apprehension of visible appearances and their successive storage as images of memory.

I'm Coming Home In Forty Days is thus concerned more with the object's syntax than with its semantics, more with the mode of perception and presentation than with whatever appears as a given fact. The representational image constituted from different viewpoints presents itself as a concept charged with the observer's experiential horizon that connects abstract impressions with subjective experience. If the film provides an extremely reduced representation of the iceberg, it casts this representation in terms of a memory riddled with the aesthetics of painting, a memory made present, yet that is still only capable of delivering back to the past those who have actually seen the image.[10]

As a trace of memorial and recollective space, this moment in time is constitutive for *I'm Coming Home in Forty Days*, which is carried by an intense temporal slowness, through which movement is derived from the image itself, rather than from a montage of the shots. Approaching painting in the a-perspectival all-over quality of their pictorial space, the slowly changing angles of view bear a trace of the referential inscription of the factual, which Roland Barthes described as the noema of photography, that insistence on the factuality of what is represented which, as it links reality with the past announces: "*the thing has been there*".[11] This insistence on a material reality and on the function of photography as the index of what was once there refers not only to the documentary moment of representation, but also to a presence separated from the passage of time

10 SEE DELEUZE, *CINEMA 2. THE TIME IMAGE* (LONDON: ATHLONE, 1989).

which has inscribed itself irrevocably within the image, beyond the simple categories of Here and Now. In film this phenomenon is joined by a new texture, not of form but of density: time, condensation in temporalization. In the successive apprehension of the iceberg, time is articulated as the pure time-image described by Gilles Deleuze as the presentation of time in which time is no longer a mere derivative of movement but rather movement becomes a perspective of time.[12] This time-image bestows on what is changing a form within which change takes place. This also means that at the very moment in which the cinematographic image comes closest to the photograph, it simultaneously distinguishes itself most radically from it, since the former represents not only time as enduring present, it is time.[13] The real is not forced to a standstill in the immediate present (which foreshadows the future), but is instead put on hold in its transitory presence. The photographic image is the result of the loss of a given moment, because it is pure presence, without duration. In opposition, the filmic image does not stop the flow of time, but supersedes it in the representation of a presence perpetually turned into the past. Although in film everything apparently takes place in the moment of now, all one sees are sequences of memories. The duration of the past is already inscribed in the present experience of film. This presence is never present at the moment, but has already come to a closure. The time of film is that of the past, staged as an illusionary present.

11 "WHAT I SEE HAS BEEN HERE, IN THIS PLACE WHICH EXTENDS BETWEEN INFINITY OF THE SUBJECT [...]; IT HAS BEEN HERE, AND YET IMMEDIATELY SEPARATED; IT HAS BEEN ABSOLUTELY, IRREFUTABLY PRESENT, AND YET ALWAYS DEFERRED." IT SHOULD BE ADDED THAT BARTHES, TOO, RECOGNIZES AN ESSENTIAL PHENOMENOLOGICAL DIFFERENCE IN THE MOVEMENT OF THE FILMIC IMAGE, ONE WHICH ITSELF REFERS, AT THE TIME OF FILMING, TO THE MOMENT OF THE FROZEN REALITY OF THE POSE. ROLAND BARTHES, *CAMERA LUCIDA, REFLECTIONS ON PHOTOGRAPHY, TRANS. RICHARD HOWARD* (NEW YORK: FARRAR, STRAUS, AND GIROUX, 1981) 76-78.

12 SEE DELEUZE, *THE TIME IMAGE*.

13 IBID, 31.

The representative function of film always stands in the way of memory as pure idea, since film has no reference to what lies outside the sign. For this reason film produces images which, in the gradual disappearance of all mimesis, occasionally present a reality entirely of their own. In *I'm Coming Home in Forty Days*, this reality presents itself as a painting transformed in slow motion that the gaze cannot grasp all at once. In its departure from geometrically oriented perspective, it demands time in order to be seen. In their succession, the various views figure together into that framework which makes possible a reconstructive cutting-off of what is seen as a visual totality, a totality which, in its complexity, can nonetheless never be fully transformed into perceptible concepts. By means of the chromatic differentiation of various shades of gray, the image takes on an opaque density that effectively thwarts any effort to differentiate depth of field. It is precisely the elimination of illusionary three-dimensionality in the mist of appearance that opens up time as a fourth dimension in which the enduring presence of the image becomes more important than its representation.

The title, with its promise "I'm Coming Home," invokes the figure of the journey, which is temporal, as well as the distance from a place to which there will be a return. The temporal moment is linked in this way with the topos of the sea voyage and its unspecific localization in a space meant to be traversed.

The ship, considered as a "rocking piece of space", as "place without place"[14] marks a condition beyond territorial fixation, a journey without any defined goal – a journey in which the idea of movement as forward movement, in the direction of concretely marked vectors, comes to a halt. Insofar as its structure is linear, the film also presents

---

14 MICHEL FOUCAULT, "ANDERE ORTE" IN: *AISTHESIS. WAHRNEHMUNG HEUTE ODER PERSPEKTIVEN EINER ANDEREN ÄSTHETIK*, EDS. KARLHEINZ BARCK, PETER GENTE, HEIDI PARIS, AND STEFAN RICHTER (LEIPZIG, 1990) 46. ALSO: *THE DOCUMENTAX-CATALOGUE*.

an abstract notion of narrativity. The ship from which the film is shot is always present, a continual rising and falling movement on the horizon, as if dictated by the waves. In this way, the barely changing image acquires a rhythmic orchestration that integrates even the position of the observer into the representation as a structuring moment of the movement.

Shifted to the foreground of the image, the first long zoom shot already disrupts, from within the image, the usual coordinates of spatial experience. As a result of the vertical tilting of the image, the vanishing point cannot be clearly determined and the pictorial space is turned into mere surface. On the other hand, this two-dimensional superficiality places the zoom firmly in the tradition of modernist painting, which dissolved the classic relationship between figure and ground, with its hierarchical ordering of the image, into radical two-dimensionality: e.g., monochromatic painting, or better yet, the "all-over" of abstract expressionism's chromatic space.

In their perceptible appearance, both iceberg and sky remain abstract entities until some of the ship's reeling enters the image as an aesthetic boundary. This boundary makes visible the location of the camera, at once the definite localization of the viewer, while making present the status of the pictorial configuration as replica. The central, second, and longest shot completes this frontal view of the iceberg with data from its stereometric dimension which are revealed during the slow trip around the iceberg. This trip stands entirely under the sign of an aesthetics of disappearance, where the boundary between iceberg and sky becomes porous and the view temporarily blurs into a visual abstract. The lead-gray color drives the space into emptiness, eliminates its coordinates and absorbs its form to the limit of the nonfigurative. All spatial fixations are set aside in favor of an untota-lizable space. Only the water appears as a smooth reflective surface, whereas the contours of the ice dissolve to the point of passing completely into the undefined realm of the sky. This diffusion becomes all the more pronounced with the boundary between water and iceberg serving as a dark line that geometrically structures the film image – almost like a horizontal "zip" whose reference to reality is continually going out of focus. In this allusion to Barnett Newman's terminology, the particular aesthetic semantics of reference belonging to *I'm Coming Home in Forty Days* is manifested.

Classic paintings like Caspar David Friedrich's *Das Eismeer (Die Gescheiterte Hoffnung)*, which begin with the subject, provide a close comparison. It is precisely in the way they differ from *I'm Coming Home in Forty Days* that they illuminate its abstract structural realism. Friedrich's blocks of ice are primarily allegorical, destroyed surface and sensual image of a landscape in upheaval. His painting provided no exact topography of nature even if the realism of his presentation gives the impression of one. In *I'm Coming Home In Forty Days*, by contrast, everything remains within the realm of the concrete, referring to nothing except what one sees. Given German Romanticism's transformation of nature into symbolic landscape, film is actually much more closely related to the formal construction of images in Abstract Expressionism. In particular, it is their affinity to the concept of the sublime that appears repeatedly when looking at the iceberg. Kant called 'sublime' that feeling which results from the boundlessness of an object, which drives the observer's experience to its outer limits and, by means of what extends beyond all reliable experience, places excessive demands on his power of judgment. Now, the actual transcendental content of what Kant calls the sublime consists in the incapacity for synthesis, an incapacity which is, at least according to Jean-François Lyotard's reading of the historical category of the aesthetic, precisely what modernist artists tried to bring forth by means of abstraction.[15] The formal reduction and deci-ded purism of the minimalists within Abstract Expressionism, such as Barnett Newman, is entirely in the service of making present the absolute by means of the transcendence of immediacy. In his text, "The Sublime is Now", Newman himself asserts programmatically that European art is concerned exclusively with the transcendence of the objective sphere, whereas American art, having freed itself from the burden of European tradition, strives toward a self-evident image which is real, concretely and universally comprehensible, and which itself presents the reality of transcendental experience. Viewed in this way, Abstract Expressionism presents itself as the history of ontological reduction only at the end of which stands the optical system of the pictorial surface. This image is not concerned with an experience, it wants to be an experience: the sublime is now. Its very content is the aesthetic presence of chromatic space, i.e. the image presents the presentation[16] as well as what occurs within it. The related claim for a fully autonomous, uninstrumentalizable art clearly refers to a metaphysical superstructure which results in the conviction that authenticity lies exclusively in unique, immediate aesthetic experience. For this reason, Newman's actual goal consisted in isolating the observer in the act of perceiving, which Newman linked with both temporal feeling and the sublime instantaneity of emotional fulfillment. The confrontation with the work is in this way nothing more than the fulfilled instant which corresponds not to measurable time, to *chronos*, but rather to the subjective experience of time and the consciousness of *kairos*. This experience implies the ideal construction of an active seeing which situates perception outside the boundaries of culture and language. In opposition to the objective world of appearance, Newman's pictorial surfaces claim to stand for the immaterial, spiritual world of pure, timeless, unchanging concepts and ideas. His works nevertheless produce an abstract effect even after the end of the postmodern heydays, since whatever

15 THIS IS AT LEAST JEAN-FRANÇOIS LYOTARD'S INTERPRETATION OF THE CRITIQUE OF JUDGMENT WHICH TURNS THE "NEGATIVE PRESENTATION" INSISTED UPON BY KANT – THE PARADOX OF A PRESEN-TATION THAT PRESENTS NOTHING – INTO THE ANNOUNCEMENT OF ABSTRACT AND MINIMALIST ART. SEE JEAN-FRANÇOIS LYOTARD, *PHILOSOPHIE UND MALEREI IM ZEITALTER IHRES EXPERIMENTIERENS* (BERLIN, 1986) 18.

16 IBID, 15.

may appear to be metaphysical in their presentation is based on a precise physical form. This form, which is determined primarily by the dimensions of what conveys the image, encompasses the observer within the large format of the chromatic space and thereby defines a precise location. In this spatially structured interaction between image and observer, in the analysis of painting's spatial conditions, lies the particular point where current artistic positions can take hold, positions which situate themselves beyond the spiritual dimension of Abstract Expressionism.

Newman's painting deals with the question of visibility, of the pheno-menology of the image, and of the role of the observer, by abstracting from contexts external to art and history. It is in this way that his painting can still serve as reference when it comes to the changing conditions for visuality in today's media age. The historically motivated demand for a strict separation between two-dimensional and three-dimensional media, between painting and sculpture, appears a thing of the past when the question of location in painting, of abstract chromatic space, is reformulated as the question of the location of painting itself.

As in Newman, one is confronted in *I'm Coming Home In Forty Days* by an insistence on the Now of perception. However, in the latter it finds an extension in the direction of minimalist aesthetics, in which the reference to transcendental presence as referential semantics is sublated into objective presence. The mode of sublimity is now articulated, as a condition for perception that dissolves duration-producing materiality in favor of what is momentary in the actual given appearance.

This is most evident in the last shot of the film, in which the per-spective is radically reversed to reveal a monochrome green surface. It has the effect of a static image, but it in fact reflects the water onto the ice in direct view so that it appears as a flat, impenetrable surface. This degree of abstraction apparently relieves the observer from the burden of searching for a reference outside the image.

Despite this, the tableau-like shot evokes an extremely reduced topography of the visible reflected in the almost painterly phenomenology of the ice, which itself provokes a state of perpetually perceiving anew. Upon closer examination, a slight eddy can be recognized running through the green surface of the water, which, as a suggestive perceptible reflection, serves ultimately to break up what is static. Through this moment of minimal movement the monochrome surface presents a legible space, i.e. it is infused with reality and can thus be related to an object. Taken up into real time, the image of the water appears to be transformed from live-image into one that is static before the structured surface of this optics allocates a material quality which would allow the static image to become an image in time. The green surface marks the peripeteia of movement at a standstill.

In this way the surface objectifies Abstract Expressionism's constitutive dialectic between process and hermeticism characterized by color surfaces that open onto the spatial dimension. The characteristic phenomenon of surface and depth – with its perceptible conversion of material surface into immaterial pictorial surface and fictive, ideal spatiality – appears here as a "getting lost" in color. Here we are dealing with nothing more than a groundbreaking trilogy of seeing, recognizing, and re-recognizing in appearance. In this last monochromatic shot, even the filtered original sounds of the soundtrack, which had reduced the sounds on location to a minimum, fall silent. In the form of a contrapuntal unification of all sounds in silence, attention is directed exclusively at what refuses to be explained beyond its visibility.

VISION IN MOTION

The last film as of yet, *Of Three Men* (1998), is a concentrate distilled
from all the previous ones, a maximum reduction surpassing the
usual aesthetics of "less is more". Shot on 35 mm, the film presents
ten minutes of unedited footage consisting of one completely static
shot of an interior. Here the cinematic apparatus is reduced to its
most minimal representative function. By means of the stationary
alignment of the camera, the time element is bound up directly with
the factor of light and indirectly with the factor of lighting. Any changes
are instantaneous and are only visible after the fact, once the
present is already past. Film fixes and conserves time as past, but
as past made present again in the process of projection, just as
the gaze of the eye of the camera is reactivated in the gaze of the
viewer. No matter how the forms of time are conjugated, they only
ever surface in the reductionist mode of the instant.[17] In this sense,
Of Three Men reflects on time and space, primarily in terms of light
as the textured materialization of time, as illumination, as transcendent appearance, and as the constitutive substance of objects.
Then there is the static darkness, concentrated by the projector's
beam of light, which elevates light to the condition for the opening-up
of the world as representation.
Significantly, there is at first nothing to see besides projected darkness.
Apparently, *Of Three Men* begins as the representation of the mere
materiality of the filmic medium, as a saturated opaque surface,
a pictorial field reduced to black projection. Yet out of the near non-
image of this blackness, the signified still speaks. This occurs as the
contours of three bodies develop schematically out of the negated
mode of replicability, until it becomes clear that the three men men-
tioned in the title are standing right in front of the camera and literally
blocking what lies behind them. When they move to the side, the
gaze opens like a stage curtain onto the interior of a Romanesque
church, which amounts to the staging of a *fiat lux* as the substrative

---

17 SEE MICHEL ONFRAY, *DIE FORMEN DER ZEIT*, 108.

condition for the perception of reality.

For Romanticism, the Christian instrumentalization of sunlight appeared not only as illumination, but also as *lux perpetua*, as eternal light and enlightenment. In the surrounding space of the church, a flat spatial conception of light predominates, which is manifested in the enormous glass windows and their modulation of the architecture. The shining through of God's light, the penetration of the walls by light, the diaphanie were all staged as an almost sensual event which served to separate the church interior from the profane and, through the play of colors and light, to transform space into a symbol for spacelessness. Even today, completely independent of its functional role, light carries the nearly universal connotation of what is transcendent.[18]

The space in *Of Three Men* is, however, no longer a church but a mosque. Pews, altars and religious objects have disappeared, the floor is covered with carpets and tacky chandeliers hang from the ceiling. Shot from a totally central perspective, the gaze of the camera is directed at the kiblah wall that marks the direction of prayer toward Mecca. This is located where the main entrance used to be. On this same wall, bright light pours in through a rose window. The spatial layout of the religious architecture, which strictly takes the altar as vanishing point, is completely turned around. Although the cloisters are still visible at the sides, they have lost their direction-determining function, since the spatial structure of the mosque,

18 THIS SUBLIME SYMBOLIC POWER OF CHRISTIAN ICONOGRAPHY WHICH IS DEMATERIALIZED IN LIGHT, IS IN THE END CONTINUED AS A SECULARIZED AESTHETIC IN THE ARTIFICIAL LIGHT-SPACES OF MINIMALISM. DAN FLAVIN AND JAMES TURRELL'S LIGHT SCULPTURES, IN WHICH LIGHT APPEARS CONCRETELY, ABSTRACTLY, AND METAPHYSICALLY, EVOKE A COMPARABLE EFFECT. FLAVIN'S NOTION OF STAGING LIGHT EVENTS WITH NORMAL, SIMPLE INDUSTRIAL LIGHTS, IS PART OF THE CONTEXT OF MINIMAL ART BECAUSE OF ITS USE OF UNLIKELY MATERIALS AND THE LOGICAL RIGOR OF ARCHITECTONIC ORDER. HIS WORKS CANNOT ELIMINATE THE METAPHYSICAL DIMENSION OF LIGHT IN SPITE OF ALL DEVELOPMENT IN THE DIRECTION OF A DE-SUBLIMATED NON-ART, AS IS AT HOME IN: *REDUCTIONIST MINIMALISM*.

in contrast to the axial layout of Christian religious buildings, is determined by the balance of the axes and the points of the compass. In the filmic representation of *Of Three Men*, the church transformed into a mosque appears as a hybridized culture figure, as a pragmatic approach to what already exists, which is made to suit a new religious context without negating the Christian origin of the building. The reason for this is that the mosque is primarily a space for prayer, and not, strictly speaking, a holy space, in which the idea of the presence of God is at work. In Islamic buildings, surface appears as mere surface, referring only to two dimensions. Likewise, space is determined not by its boundaries, but rather is defined as a place without any predetermined, overarching symmetric order, without center or vanishing point.

Yet the monocular central perspective of the camera forces the decentralized structure of the mosque back into the Western tradition of perspectival space with its understanding of what it means to see.[19] In the way perspective has been constructed since the Italian Renaissance, the intended observer, as the subject of the constructed picture, finds himself in the vanishing point of the vectors of sight. This perspectival construction of visual space extends pictorial space into the space in front of the picture, wherein the observer discovers that ideal position in which the discrepancy between image production and impressions of reality appear suspended in favor of the reality currently being constituted by the picture. In *Of Three Men*, central perspective and pictorial symmetry both figure as a reference to pictorial ideas concerning the geometric ordering of the visible, in which the conventions of perspective

---

19 SEE NORMAN BRYSON, *VISION AND PAINTING. THE LOGIC OF THE GAZE* (LONDON, 1983). FOR THE AFFINITY BETWEEN THE MONOCULAR PERSPECTIVAL CONSTRUCTION AND THE MACHINIC OPTICS OF THE CAMERA, COMPARE ARGUMENTS BY FILM THEORISTS LIKE CHRISTIAN METZ, JEAN BAUDRY, AND STEPHEN HEATH. SEE ALSO KAJA SILVERMAN'S SYNTHESIZING ACCOUNT, "WHAT IS A CAMERA? OR: HISTORY IN THE FIELD OF VISION" IN: *DISCOURSE 15:3* (SPRING 1993) 3-38.

presuppose a static, monocular understanding of what it means to see. The experience of space and reality moves exclusively within this preformed system, which is itself used as an instrumental medium of perception.

In realistic painting, as in film, the idealist notion of perception is based on a perspectival gaze that figures as the condition for a convincing reduplication of the world. The logic behind this gaze consists in a reduction of the body of the producer of the image, as well as that of the observer, to one single point on the eye's retina, thereby situating what is captured on the canvas outside all duration in time. As a punctual instant, this idealized gaze is a hypothetical attempt to isolate one moment of motionlessness from the continuum of seeing and of time. This gaze thus corresponds to the mechanical optics of the camera, which substitutes the subject with a preformation of the subject's sight; it delegates the role of the eye to the objective lens and – as the projection of the self and the occupation of the world by the "I" – positions itself (in the tradition of Cartesian logic) as the omniscient centralized subject. On the level of the imaginary, the observer of the perspectival construction is always already included in the picture, since he finds himself at the center of an artifact that reproduces reality. Equally negated in the process are both the act of seeing in its duration and the awareness of the time in which the image is produced. However, a "metaphysics of presence" [20] in the service of an illusion of reality, such as this one, is contradicted by the factual maneuverability of the seeing eye, which can only concentrate, in its focal points, on one part of the picture at a time. In opposition to the construct of a gaze capable of grasping everything all at once, which elevates the painted / filmed image to the status of presence, this seeing does not take place in an instant but rather in the duration of observation.

20 BRYSON, *THE LOGIC OF THE GAZE*, 89FF.

Of Three Men reduces the interior of the mosque to its central perspectival view, giving the duration of seeing back to the gaze. The eye of the camera remains static, yet the eye of the observer has endless time to study the projection. Although movement and development are controlled through a number of conceptual specifications (e.g., placement of the camera, filming time), time itself is liberated from its objectification of the present. With this, *Of Three Men* returns to the earliest days of film history: not a movement-image but an image in movement, distinguished less by its state than by its tendency.[21] Only the changing light asserts itself as intensity of movement and extension in the space. In this minimal movement within the image reproduced by the camera lies the particular challenge of the filmic principle, when within its dispositive structure an extremely sensual painting is constituted that exists in time.

Within the medium of film, the mosque appears as both illuminating and illuminated architecture, as a sculptural projection room receiving its light from an external source. As a sculptor of light, the room effectively intensifies, steers, controls, and forms it. Only the light pouring in through the round window at the center of the image can be identified as a direct source of light. By contrast, the sunlight streaming in through the side windows appears as a phenomenal event. In the measure that it recalls the continual transition of reality, this light transforms the mosque into a model for perception in which the sense of proportion and of seeing itself is altered. Since, ultimately, the isomorphism between the structure of space and that of perception is such that the everyday patterns of perception are not repeated but rather broken by a restructuring of space that assaults the conventions of seeing. The interior is contingent on the outside, which means that what can be seen follows from what cannot be seen. Change is exclusively dependent on the external

21 SEE DELEUZE, *THE MOVEMENT-IMAGE.*

play of light that stages the other within the aleatory realm of the extraordinary. Movement is created only by changes in the incoming light, by changes in the shadows, textures, even by the disappearing three-dimensionality of things.

Understood in its double coding as both *lux* and *lumen*, as both physical and metaphysical, light is the transcendental condition for sensual ideation, for aesthetic representation, and is the prerequisite for the visible in both its visibility and its replication. Light always forgoes a connection to darkness as its negation, against which it defines itself as intensity. In its constant change, light is also a representation of a realistic, invisible time that, as a continuum liberated from all meaning, conceals itself behind the appearance of indestructible duration.

Light's time appears circular, since it is induced and determined by the course of the sun. When the sun shines through or disappears behind a cloud, it produces both a quantitative and chromatic modification that affects the perception of space and its objects, and it thereby elevates the changing play of light to both measure and evidence the passing of time. Weather is the visible, immanent, and aesthetic variation of passing time, whether regular or circular. As the meteorological form of time, weather crosses through time's continuum. In the rhythm of day and night everything returns with a calculable regularity that is part of a logic that knows no probability, but which subsists, rather, on certainties. Meteorological time, on the other hand, is purely aleatory and modulates light and shadow in unpredictable ways.[22] In *Of Three Men*, time is made materially visible only in the colorful variations of light. Hence when circular time is visualized by means of aleatory time, it also means that the texture of the former is nothing but the expansion of the latter.[23]

---

22 AND SINCE THE WEATHER IS SO UNPREDICTABLE, THE LIGHT SOURCES IN THE MOSQUE ARE NOT COMPLETELY NATURAL, BUT RATHER SLIGHTLY MANIPULATED – FILMIC RECONSTRUCTION PRODUCING CONDITIONS THAT ARE AS CLOSE AS POSSIBLE TO NATURAL LIGHT.

Yet the ontology of time also demonstrates that time can be transformed, slowed down, modified and formed. Even if time can be defined as the irreversible relationship of succession, it is nevertheless perceived differently both objectively and subjectively.

In order to be made visible, time as an idea must be artificially spatialized, whereas in experience it is articulated outside of chronometric structures. In film, time is experienced primarily as movement, as the sequence of distinct moments that pass by the eye. Paradoxically, film conforms to the object's time while simultaneously recording its duration.[24]

De Rijke and de Rooij slow the tempo down to "real time" and, in the parallel link between perception time and filming time, bring what is seen back to perception. In doing so, their films free themselves from the reality constraints of the shot, the block of homogeneous time – which André Bazin declared the guarantee of realism – which determines the ontology of the filmic image. Instead, a nearly irrevocable difference is produced between the subjective sense of time and the time of the film, in which the experience of time in the flow of images is never the same as the individual experience of time in the real. This is paradoxical, since *Of Three Men* is filmed in real time, and its ten-minute duration corresponds exactly to the ten minutes in which it was filmed. Yet the way the medium is viewed is so conditioned by its own temporal reality, consisting in speeding up and slowing down, that the modifications of light are precisely what serve as an indexical representation of time and suggest an extreme slowing down of real time. *Of Three Men* has its own rhythm which differs from ours simply because it translates what is in fact there into another medium. Time in *Of Three Men* is meditative whereas ours is chronographic. This irrevocable difference plays an essential role in its reception since time in the film is no longer that of the

23 SEE ONFRAY, *FORMEN DER ZEIT,* 51FF.

24 SEE BAZIN, *QU'EST-CE QUE C'EST LE CINÉMA?,*151.

event, but rather that of aesthetic experience. Aesthetic experience occurs in the mode of present contemplation, in which the nature of the event in aesthetic time does not necessarily relate in a referential way to the events in reality.

"Real-time" movies such as this one employ a stationary camera positioned in front of an object in order to present the eternity of time as the staging of aesthetic experience. They call to mind Andy Warhol's *Empire*, an 8-hour silent film about the Empire State Building in New York, in which nothing occurs besides minimal changes in the play of light, the encroaching darkness, and the artificial lighting of the building. Shot from the 44th floor of a facing building, Warhol's film shows an almost unchanging view of the Empire State Building until, hours later, the glass and steel Art-Deco monument sinks, with the setting sun, into obscurity and meaninglessness. In the end, the two-dimensional image, consisting only in darkness and light, completely loses its referential relation to reality and appears to be transformed into the pure materiality of the filmic image. In its epic length and unwavering renunciation of any intervention beyond the choice of camera angle, *Empire* is the absolute homage to time as pure duration, to the irreducible passing of time. Despite its obsessive fixation on the building, *Empire* has as little to do with that object as it does with chronometric time. In its reduction to only what can be seen, the film effectively substitutes chronology and story with the process of watching, since there is nothing invisible behind the visible image of the skyscraper that could suddenly appear and retrospectively provide things with their desired meaning. Moreover, *Empire* produces a view defining frame, behind which there is no alternative reality: the absolute frame of the image as a materiality without substance.

In this radical provocation of conventional cinema – as a locus of stories, diversions, and spectacles – Warhol marked off an ontological terrain for film, in which film, abstracted from all figurativeness, constitutes the particular medium of aesthetic experience. It is precisely in their simple duration that Warhol's interminable films alter perception. Perception initially waits for something to happen, but then trades in the apparent constancy of the image for a perspective of minimal change in what is de facto the same.[25] In this absolute opposition of duration to chronological time, the film orchestrates the temporalization of observation and the attention of the gaze in the form of a fixation of perception per se. The viewing of Warhol's films becomes the endless observation of one's own act of watching. This is a radical rejection of the efforts of cinematography to dissolve the superficiality of the image in favor of the reality allegedly lying beneath it, and, by doing so, negating seeing-time as the decoding of its signs. What is attractive in the suspension of the spatial dimension, with its geometric perspective, lies in the suspension of time by duration, in the exchange of the time of reason for the time of intensity. Time becomes qualitative duration when the spatial and temporal dimensions attain a contemporariness that can be intuitively perceived. This intuitive impression of temporal duration is expressed as the continuity of flow, which can only be perceived as the unity, never as the successive sequence of distinct moments. Perceived time is itself turned into pure movement, in which no rigid things exist, "only becoming things, no circumstances, only changing circumstances".[26]

25 WARHOL'S FILMS LIKE *EAT* (1963, 29 MIN.), *SLEEP* (1963, 321 MIN.), *KISS* (1963, 50 MIN.) OR *EMPIRE* (1964, 485 MIN.) DEMONSTRATE ONLY WHAT THE TITLE INDICATES: SOMEONE EATS, SOMEONE SLEEPS, PEOPLE KISS. THE ORIGINAL CHALLENGE OF THESE EXCEEDINGLY LONG FILMS RESTED IN THEIR BEING SHOWN AS MOVIES IN THE THEATER – WHAT IS THE AUDIENCE TO DO, WHEN IT SITS DOWN FULL OF EXPECTATIONS, WHEN ALL THERE IS TO SEE ON THE SCREEN IS JUST ABOUT THE SAME THING? ASIDE FROM WARHOL'S INTENT THAT THE RECEPTION OF THE FILM WAS ITSELF A "HAPPENING", THERE IS ALSO THE SET OF AESTHETIC RULES PARTICULAR TO FILMIC MATERIAL, WHICH AFFORDS AN ANALYSIS OF A FILMIC TIME INDEPENDENT OF THE CONTEXT OF THE MOVIE THEATER. WARHOL'S FILMS FUNCTION PERFECTLY IN THE CONTEXT OF THE EXHIBITION, AS DOUGLAS GORDON'S BOOTLEG EMPIRE VERSION OF *EMPIRE*, WHICH AS AN HOMAGE TO WARHOL'S WORK PUSHED THE FILM INTO THE CONTEXT OF ART RECEPTION AND LINKED THE TEMPORAL MOMENT OF VIEWING WITH THE CATEGORY OF THE AESTHETIC.

In *Of Three Men*, there is only movement within space as the light's intensity of movement. In fact, the interior of the mosque is presented as a snapshot beyond decidedly conceptual considerations to translate an abstract idea into a prefabricated dramaturgy. As a mere affirmation of space and the phenomenology of its sensual appearance, *Of Three Men* knows no finality; everything could simply continue forever as it is. Seen in this way, the film presents nothing more than ten minutes from the continuum of time and light, and thereby nothing more than the ontology of the filmic in its purest form.

26 HENRI BERGSON, *DENKEN UND SCHÖPFERISCHES WERDEN* (FRANKFURT/M., 1985) 211.

POST-MINIMAL PROJECTIONS
(INSIDE AND OUTSIDE THE FRAME)

The connection of painting to cinema, as de Rijke/de Rooij practice it, neither strives to claim the ideal of a new filmic intermediacy, nor to force a de-differentiation of the arts through a synthesis of various aesthetics. It also has nothing to do with generalizing the character of the medium of film. Rather, behind the works of de Rijke/de Rooij lies the insight that the filmic apparatus represents a juxtaposition of aesthetic, discursive, and technological factors that allow various forms of articulation. Film as art – the thought that has dominated the medium since its earliest days – is given new form. De Rijke/de Rooij do so by not allowing art to be subsumed under the *dispositif* "cinema"; on the contrary, they present their films explicitly in the context of institutionalized art and thereby place them in a discursive field which takes other criteria, external to film, as its referential framework.

One of these referents is manifested as the heir to American Minimalism, or rather, as the post-minimalist seizure of the real as a parameter of the perception of time and space. Connected to that is the implication of *presence*, which had increasingly gained meaning in the operational fields of the fine arts. Proceeding from the Minimal Art of the late sixties, which submitted the relation between work and viewer as well as the superimposition of time, space, and movement to a formalist redefinition, its concept of "presence and place" moved into the center of artistic practice.[27] With the clear-cut positioning of minimalist object-art, the viewer was denied the sovereign space of classical art for the sake of the Here and Now of the work's presence. Avoiding any reference outside of themselves, the works of Minimal Art thus evoke a new kind of experience of presence, in which the categorical determination of the sculpture was given a new function; it influenced the behavior of the viewer, which was only possible as such if a continuity of space existed, in which object and recipient were constituted to the same degree.

---

27 SEE GEORG STEMMRICH (ED.), *MINIMAL ART – A CRITICAL RETROSPECTIVE* (DRESDEN, BASEL: 1997) 12.

It no longer related only formally to the work's surface as an expression of its media or material qualities, but also to an ascertainment of the perceptible consequences of its intervention within a determined space.[28] In confronting the objects of Minimalism, the viewer was practically forced to develop a consciousness for his own physicality in relation to the work of art. As opposed to phenomenological concepts of visibility, it was always the material structure of the object that in Minimal Art served as the conceptual basis for visuality and was supposed to allow the viewer a consciousness of his or her own position in the visible. In reflecting the time-components of perception, he or she thus had to grant a special status to the coordinates of time and space when treating the work according to its material completion. In this way, Minimalism raised questions of time in art that were diametrically opposed to the understanding of Modernism, particularly Abstract Expressionism, with its notion of the work of art as present and graspable in one glance. Whereas the transcendental moment was categorically replaced by the duration of beholding. Within the conceptual dichotomy of materiality and visuality, the question of a new positioning of art in the visible thus became important; this question still bears currency beyond the paradigms of Minimal Art.[29] In post-minimalist art this aspect survives despite the diversified character of artistic production

---

28 AMERICAN MINIMALISM BREAKS WITH THE TRADITION OF IDEALISM, EVEN IF IT AFFIRMS THE PURE FORM AND LOGICAL STRUCTURE OR LENDS A FORMAL GESTALT TO ABSTRACT THOUGHTS. FOR IT IS PRECISELY THE METAPHYSICAL DUALISM OF SUBJECT AND OBJECT THAT MINIMALISM ATTEMPTS TO OVERCOME IN THE PHENOMENOLOGICAL EXPERIENCE OF THE WORK. IN SO DOING, THE WORK OF MINIMAL ART MAKES THE PURITY OF THE CONCEPT MORE COMPLICATED THROUGH A CERTAIN CONTIGENCY OF PERCEPTION. IN THE END, ANALYSIS STEMMING FROM THE DIRECTION OF MINIMAL ART MOVES MORE TOWARDS EPISTEMOLOGY THAN TOWARDS ONTOLOGY, AS IT IS MORE CONCERNED THE CONDITIONS OF PERCEPTION AND THE BORDERS OF CONVENTION WITHIN ART THAN WITH THE FORMAL ESSENCE AND CATEGORICAL BEING. SEE HAL FOSTER, "DIE CRUX DES MINIMALISMUS" IN: ED. STEMMRICH, *MINIMAL ART*, 599FF.

29 IBID, 29.

and the departure from coherent form toward plural concepts under modified prerequisites – space and time were and still are the determining parameters of many works on the semantic as well as material levels.

In its formal analysis of perception and of the confrontation between "known constants and experienced variation" (per Robert Morris), Minimalism also confronted the conditions of perception as a dissociation of perception and knowledge through a reduction to concrete parameters. Above all, it shares with film (which reflects on its own mechanical status) this interest in bringing together the representation of the presumably known with a perception of it as something unknown. Thus, the cinematic exploration of artistic praxis – in the tradition of the self-reflexively structural but also conceptual cinema – indirectly questions forms of perception according to their modeling by forms of images. Given the way in which film replicates the world, it represents itself directly as a syntax for understanding the world; that is, the interest in the image is also a new formation of the real, bound to filmic logic that in spite of all abstraction still moves within the paradigms of the pictorial.

Despite a specific spatial interest, as well as the creation of defined environments as such, the works of de Rijke/de Rooij stand out for their lack of materiality; as films, they consist mostly of projected light in space. Insofar as they structurally insist on time and space, these works reconfigure the raw matter of time-space parameters. The awareness of dimensions as determinants of the cinematic illusion emerges primarily on the semantic level and is articulated as a principle: space and time are plastically visible categories in the works of de Rijke/de Rooij. Therein lies a decisive difference from conventional film, which seeks to sublate itself as an object in the complete illusion of reference and thereby negate itself in its own materiality. However, this technological, mechanical dimension of the filmic achieves visibility with de Rijke/de Rooij, who demand a precise mode of watching. By replacing the framing function, usually performed by the edges of the screen, with framing within the image, and by projecting their films on a white wall rather than on a screen, they aim for an imaginary separation of apparatus and image. Only the surface of the wall around the projected image forms a frame to divide it from the architectural space. An optical difference always remains between a painting mimetically reproducing the real, the appearance of the image, and the materials of its function. The film's image, on the contrary, lacks this recognizable difference between the material of the image and the image itself, even if the field of the image on the screen lends the projection a certain object-like quality. On the one hand, this leads to a dematerialization of the projection of light, which still additionally lacks, in de Rijke/de Rooij's work, the *passepartout* of the delineating cinema curtain. On the other hand, it also involves a materialization of the entire "white cube", not merely the environment, but also the concrete locus of the filmic image. This room that does not intend to simulate a movie theater but instead takes over its concentrated atmosphere minimizes the dispositive objectification of filmic discourse. Furthermore, it emphasizes the material structure of the filmic apparatus precisely because it integrates into the presentation not only the referential dimension of the representation of visible reality, but also the essential character of film as projected light-image. The external framing of de Rijke/de Rooij's films is presented as a hybrid figure, connecting the formal structure of cinema with the spatial interventions of minimalist sculpture. Even when the film is not being projected, the space to which it belongs still exists. Next to the factor of time, which differentiates the medium of film from all other material arts, it is mainly the inevitable end of the projection time that raises it to a conceptual construct; the absence of the image and the memory of that which just occurred also includes the time following its actual presence in the frame of the work. The aesthetic of disappearance necessarily transforms the immaterial substance of the light-image into a fading memory, the impression of the image nevertheless survives as a memory trace.

Accordingly, the substantial moment of the cinematic, the temporal frame of projection, attains an explicit status in its contextualization in the art-system. As an analogous image medium, the works of de Rijke and de Rooij possess a precise temporal definition, which is not least of all determined by the ontological condition that film must have a beginning and an end. Their works are not projected as an infinite loop, but rather as self-contained screenings, which occur in specified intervals (see appendix). Thus, the work and its beholding demand their own time, which the public is forced to take.

Aside from the recourse to minimalist positions regarding the form of the presentation as a frame for the film, the film itself is still positioned in a frame of references adapted from art. In particular, de Rijke/ de Rooij's works are determined by the norms of painting and a relation to other "time-based" arts.

The medium of film is presented in these works in terms of its material specificity as well as its perceptual potential. Because the film's narrative is directly bound to the material conditions of the filmic production of meaning, the mimetic discourse of cinema enters the sphere of the self-critical discourse of modernity. Yet this juxtaposition of filmic reality and the self-referentiality of modernist visuality is but one of many aspects affecting both of the early films, *Chun Tian* and *Forever and Ever*. At the very least, these films still participate marginally in the framework of filmic narration, although less on the thematic than on the formal level. In other words, they do not present any plot-driven thematics, but rather it is a filmic structure which first produces the actual topic, even if it is only in the empty space between the images. The fact that the topic lacks an object leads to the thematization of form, of movement, and of the perception of the real within the illusionary space of film. It is important not to forget that filmic representation is not merely prefigured by perceptual dispositions, but it must also submit to the norms of an historically sanctioned aesthetic. When the medium of film is subjected to close scrutiny as a technological production of *images*, the challenge to the dialectics between film and mechanical optics shifts decisively into painting's frame of visual reference.

This recourse to painting as a paradigm of determining the visual is most productive when it attempts to lead film back to those pictorial traditions in which film moves as an image medium but against which it also tries to delineate itself aesthetically. In the end, it is precisely the application of visual principles of composition to the filmic construct, and the interference of the norms of the static and the moving filmic image, which bring forth a difference between the traditional and the technological production of images. This difference is not merely motivated by a production aesthetic, but also concerns the relation of mechanical conditions to various forms of seeing.

This in no way means that the transfer of the epistemological potential derived from art has to occur merely in a self-referential discourse that elevates the difference between perception and apperception to a major issue. It is much more the case that film, on the heels of painting, also encounters its own foundations, which do not necessarily promote it to the heights of modernist aesthetics as a technological, mechanical medium of image production. Although the fundamental prohibition against the illusory depth and perspectival vanishing point of the Renaissance characterizes the discourse of modern painting, the narrative cinema of illusions is marked precisely by the activation of the classic illusory means of producing spatial structures. Narrative film strives for three-dimensional effects as a negation of the real two-dimensionality of the film's image in order to give the impression of reality. As representational structuring, framing and depth of field point to the conventions of representation found in classical painting. These conventions, broken by modern art, are primary functions of the formal-aesthetic repertoire of narrative film. Whereas the prohibition against represented depth consequently led to the thematization of two-dimensionality in nonfigural painting, the medium of film, seen in this way, seemed to fall anachronistically behind the aesthetic achievements of Modernism.[30] Only after the differentiation of film as the medium which breaks convention and operates self-reflexively on the filmic meta-level does it gain its potential to abstract from mere resemblance in the context of artistic production and reception. This does not merely imply instrumentalizing cinematography as a medium for reflecting on artistic praxis or turning away from the representation of the real in the dissolution of the filmic image into the graphic surface.

In the works of de Rijke/de Rooij, the rhetoric of film is connected once again to painting in order to submit its components – format, proportion, perspective, and composition – to a renewed questioning. Their grasp of reality remains thoroughly phenomenological; the visible reality indeed appears to be an image preformed by painterly tradition, but there are nevertheless no recourses to painting directly motivated by the history of art, nor are there any direct citations aimed at recognition. Certain shots are indeed handled like painting; however, the tableau-like shots are not exhausted as they point to specific analogies to pictorial composition from the archives of art. On the contrary, their historical achievements, elevated to film's point of departure, turn these composed shots into the products of the very thing which they are not. De Rijke/de Rooij refer solely to an abstract scaffolding, which they distill from the historical spatial sensibilities as well as from the monochrome color fields of Modernism. Thus, the often symmetrical construction of the image, the deployment of plan-tableaux, and the staring camera with its central perspective and symmetry of images, figure as references to pictorial notions of a geometrical ordering of the visible. They also refer to the systematization of the visual since the Renaissance, with its pictorial norms

30 SEE YVONNE SPIELMANN, "FRAMING, FADING, FAKE: PETER GREENAWAYS KUNST DER REGELN"

IN: JOACHIM PAECH, ED., *FILM, FERNSEHEN, VIDEO UND DIE KUNST* (STUTTGART, 1994) 132–149.

(such as the construction of perspective). De Rijke/de Rooij's films completely ignore the potential of a subjective, personified camera. Their systematized observer-position always remains bound to a clearly defined aesthetic limit. Even the field of the image is a geometrical, closed system along selected coordinates. In these spatial compositions, consisting of horizontal and vertical lines, every movement has a fixed place. The geometrical conception of the field of the image grants a predetermined frame for everything that is inscribed within it.[31] Moreover, the distancing function of the frame repeatedly appears in the film's picture. As a duplication within the image, by means of geometric structures or architectonic configurations, it sets new frames within the actual framing of the shot.[32] This moment of the visible limit of the image emphasizes the distance already produced by the tracking of the camera, which is reduced to the description of vertical lines; its repetition and accentuation dissolves the difference between the filmic image and the painted panel.

The frame of a painting encloses a space indicating an inwardly directed, centripetal orientation, whereas the filmic tableau is contained by a mask presented as a limit to vision virtually opened to the outside by the momentum of the movement.[33] Created by the angle of view, this frame of the image figures as a delimitation of

31 SEE GILLES DELEUZE, *CINEMA 1. THE MOVEMENT-IMAGE* (MINNEAPOLIS: U. OF MINNESOTA PRESS, 1983) WITH HIS FUNDAMENTAL DIFFERENTIATION BETWEEN THE GEOMETRICAL AND PHYSICAL FIELD OF THE IMAGE. THE GEOMETRICAL FIELD OF THE IMAGE DEFINES WHAT MOVES IN IT; THE PHYSICAL FIELD OF THE IMAGE IS PRESENTED AS A DYNAMIC CONSTRUCTION CONCEIVED IN DIRECT DEPENDENCE ON THE SCENE, THE FIGURES, AND THE OBJECTS.

32 IN THEIR FILMS, THERE IS ALWAYS A FRAME VISIBLY BROUGHT INTO THE IMAGE WITH AESTHETIC LIMITS IN FORM. FOR EXAMPLE, THE VERTICAL BALCONY RAILINGS IN *FOREVER AND EVER* OR THE SHIP'S RIGGING WHICH KEEPS SUDDENLY APPEARING IN: THE IMAGE IN *I'M COMING HOME IN FORTY DAYS*.

33 SEE ANDRÉ BAZIN, "PEINTURE ET CINÉMA" IN: *QU'EST-CE QUE LE CINÉMA*. ÉDITION DÉFINITIVE (PARIS, 1981) 188.

space and privileges classifications as well as structurings of the real. The delimitation of the images thus means the discovery of a frame defining the very view which should figure as the image of the camera and of the projection. When the filmic image claims to be the real itself, however, it normally attempts to negate the fact that it has a frame. It goes to great pains to use the fragmentary view to represent the manifold, and to use the self-betraying view to stage reality with the omnipotence of the gaze. If it is not to be reminiscent of painting, the delimiting frame lets the process of view-finding disappear in the result of the filmic image; conversely, it could elevate the edge of the image to a function pointing beyond the current image and into the one following it as a visibly invisible one.

In de Rijke/de Rooij's filmic constructions, this outwardly directed construction of the image is repeatedly put into question by the visible setting of the view as a delimiting pattern. Through such antagonisms, which are not synthesizable to a higher level, the system of the image emerges plastically as it defines representation. The extremely long shots of their films also introduce additional parameters, which shift the emphasis – by means of which the filmic image can be recognized as a constructed artifact – from the visible to the invisible, the unstructured totality behind the structured space. It also becomes evident that space only exists as a terrain of the field of vision that appropriates geometry, as the optical illusion of a another dimension. Aside from the soundtrack, which does not serve the purpose of filmic realism in de Rijke/de Rooij's work,[34] film limits itself to the perceptible qualities of things presented in a dematerialized state, transformed into pure visibility without substance.

There is another category – perhaps in contradistinction to the above – which, as an abstract quality, determines the aesthetic of their films: the truly filmic moment of time. Film indeed consists of countless separate images, but it appears as a visual continuum – a continuum like the one that determines seeing. Thus, film significantly differs from photography and painting, in which time is concentrated in a still moment. Photography isolates a moment of the real from the flow of time, whereas painting, in its own mode of representation, develops a categorically different conception of duration. Even when one speaks of the filmic image, it is not at all, in the real sense, an image in which the continuum of time, brought to a halt, finds expression. On the contrary, film first develops out of the negation of the concept of the image as a static construct. Film does not only use the increase in the abstraction of the senses which it possesses over the image; it also uses time's materialization in movement. It obtains its plastic effect of depth by using time, and time is itself reproduced as perspective in film.[35]

What characterizes de Rijke/de Rooij's films is precisely the reduction of cineastically manipulated movement. (Almost) everything occurs in real time. In both of their latest works – *I'm Coming Home in Forty Days* and *Of Three Men* – the filmic is primarily derived from the visible difference from those other images which do not even change with time. This difference between the static and the moving image is normally formulated with such clarity that it will at first not be perceived at all if the affinity to the static image is semantic and not structural – and is, in the latter case, superimposed, in the permutation of accelerated time, with other filmic images.

---

34 IN NONE OF DE RIJKE/DE ROOIJ'S FILMS IS THERE A DIRECT DIEGETIC CONNECTION BETWEEN IMAGE AND SOUND, AND IN MANY CASES THERE IS NO SOUND AT ALL. FOR THE MOST PART, THERE ARE DIALOGUES AND NOISES FROM OFF-CAMERA; THEY CAN ONLY BE CONSIDERED IMAGINARILY TO BE PART OF THE CURRENTLY VISIBLE. IN CHUN TIAN, THERE ARE ONLY VOICES FROM OFF-CAMERA, AS IN *FOREVER AND EVER*, IN WHICH THE ANNOYING RINGING OF A TELEPHONE PLAYS A CENTRAL ROLE ALTHOUGH THE TELEPHONE IS NEVER TO BE SEEN. AT THE END OF THE FILM, WHEN THE PEOPLE VISIBLY SPEAK, IT IS ALMOST IRRITATING. IN *I'M COMING HOME IN FORTY DAYS*, THE SOUND HAS BEEN RADICALLY DROPPED AND THE REAL SETTING'S SOUNDS HAVE BEEN MONTAGED INTO A MINIMALIST SOUNDTRACK. *OF THREE MEN* BEGINS WITH NOISES WHICH ARE ALMOST TOO LOUD AND ENDS WITH ALMOST NO SOUND AT ALL.

35 SEE DELEUZE, *THE MOVEMENT-IMAGE*.

The productive question repeatedly arises anew, precisely in light of the ubiquity of images from the mass media: what, then, is an image? In their filmic code, the mass media images themselves always indirectly reflect their own status in the field of the visible. In de Rijke/de Rooij's work, this postponement and condensation of the real, effected in the representational process, does not occur with digital video, but rather in the classic analogue of film. What is being made a topic in their films that present abstract models of reality are also the specific qualities of a traditional medium as a model for the production of images. The analogue film – as a guarantee of a halfway referent to a previous original – stands in opposition to the digital video image, which connotes ephemerality, the converse of which is to be found in the notion of the quality of duration apparently granted by film to that which is seen. In a purely material sense, film fixates what is perceived to a greater degree than video, in even better quality. Video, on the other hand, is supposed to be the medium that can render visible what is actually not visible – by slowing down or speeding up images, by coarsening the framework, superimposing and reversing, phasing and digitally treating everything that is mechanically fixed. Video objectifies the illusion of the visible to the degree that its electronic images practically presuppose their manipulability, undecidability, and inauthenticity.

It is one of the basic presuppositions of cinema as dispositif that the filmic image appears to be the real itself, that it constitutes, as Roland Barthes formulates, a "perfect analogy" to reality.[36] The monocular gaze of the camera does not simulate reality but rather the position of the subject. At the very least, the belief in the appearance of reality as the real itself must therefore be at hand so that film fulfills the criterion of resemblance. On the other hand,

36 ROLAND BARTHES, "DIE FOTOGRAFIE ALS BOTSCHAFT" IN: *DER ENTGEGENKOMMENDE UND DER STUMPFE SINN. KRITISCHE ESSAYS III* (FRANKFURT/M., 1990) 13.

this appearance of the analogy leads to the thematization of seeing in itself, for film is not the radical Other of perception but rather is tied in to the visual experience of reality according to its structure in agreement with our culture. In this sense, film represents the Other within the Self as a special case of the deconstruction of the gaze and the image.[37] In the cinematographic process of resembling, in the (re)production of the analogous as mechanical appearance, something occurs; the extra-filmic, "real" experience of seeing, as a given of the gaze and of the image, is subjected to a permanent questioning of its reality content. And out of this questioning, the experience of seeing can never emerge completely unscathed. Film deconstructs our concept of reality; it leads it into the trajectories of metonymy, where for a split second everything that is shown loses its tried-and-true significance. Film promises reality yet only delivers one possible reality in the camera's selective gaze.

We are aware of this, yet the seduction of cinema does everything in its power to make us forget this fact for the sake of creating a reality effect of the symbolic order, in which what happens on the screen is legitimized. In this paradox of closeness through distance, the film and the viewer can only ever constitute an imaginary unity, never truly attainable, the basis of which is the reference to reality. By duplicating reality, the filmic image dissolves the concept of a single reality in the same way that it dissolves space with its absorption of time. The field of the image does engage with the real, but forces it into a peculiar coexistence with its filmic double and creates a configuration in which the real and its technological duplicate are no longer referential, like photography, but rather coupled with each other temporally and therefore structurally.

While considering the cinematic shift in the real – in which the surface of the things does not reveal what the things are but rather only how

37 SEE MICHAEL KÖTZ, *DER TRAUM, DAS SEHEN UND DAS KINO. FILM UND WIRKLICHKEIT DES IMAGINÄREN* (FRANKFURT/M. 1986).

they are perceived – de Rijke/de Rooij are only concerned
with cinematography in a narrower sense: the limits of the images,
camera perspective, depth of field, camera movement, architecture,
and lighting. Because the medium is immediately linked with the
performance due to its categorical double reality, de Rijke/de Rooij
are mainly interested in the difference between film and reality,
the loss of three-dimensionality, the limited field of the image, the
montage, and the lack of acoustic and other sensory impressions.
They use this difference to put filmic reproduction in direct tension
with reproduced reality. The mode of duplication becomes an
aesthetic intervention within the field of the visible.

By integrating formal and semiotic distance into the filmic representational structure, de Rijke/de Rooij also approach the concrete
form of what is objective, which film as film appears to render transparent in its aesthetic quality as a sign. Their filmic discourse (for film
is always the world transformed into discourse) places the emphasis
on the specific perception of reality in its mediated transformation.
They therefore never completely negate the material specificity of
film; instead, they present it in the deconstruction of the "reality
effect", which is nothing more than a world of two-dimensional images
pretending to be the real. The fact that the objectifying power of the
filmic apparatus stands in opposition to the idea of a direct access
to reality becomes the aesthetic principle. This also implies a
distancing from the primacy of what is to be seen in favor of a turn
to the perceiving gaze in itself. Contemplation, in de Rijke/de Rooij's
films, thus always remains a conscious analysis of images, even if
these images only conditionally indicate an outside world that they
represent. The colors of their films are somehow always either
too colorful or too dull; in any case, they do not appear to have
been taken immediately from the world outside, while still not having
a synthetic effect. The views are pictorial views, contradicting the
conventional gaze, even if they are not directly alienating. Thus, the
real obtains a visual substance that derives its potential precisely

from the difference to the usually visual. Preprogrammed perceptual faculties are irritated, but the alienation intervenes only in a limited manner in relation to the real. What becomes more noticeable are the effects of the distancing, the abstract approach to the medium as a agency of depiction, and the temporality of perception as a central category of the filmic, now shifted into a new context for questioning the conditions of this perception.

Nevertheless, even this linkage of film to the category of autonomous art has a difficult time escaping the prerequisites of the cinematic. Both the alignment of contemplation to the (self-)conscious reception oriented to the work of art, and the reflective vision essentially bound to form always bear, in all abstraction, the residual traces of the illusionary machine that determines the essence of cinema. Eventually, one still succumbs to the fascination of the other reality.

In de Rijke/de Rooij's works, there is therefore a recurrent formal element that converts the fascination with the filmic as a sensual quality of the perceived image into a conceptual construct – they always end with a sudden cut, an unexpected breaking-off of the project "film". This ending behaves as a counterpoint and – from the perspective of the audience – is counterproductive to the actual rhythm of the images, which it abruptly interrupts. As a productive disobedience toward the rhetoric of finality, their films thus preserve the fragmentary character that only then finds its completion when the wall becomes empty after the end of the projection. This conceptual emptiness, integral to the work, elevates the absence of the image to a positive component of itself. Seeing the emptiness after the end of the film thus also means integrating into perception exactly what belongs there but is absent, and thus perceiving the absence of the lack as a quality of the present.

NICOLAUS SCHAFHAUSEN: INTERVIEW MIT DE RIJKE/DE ROOIJ
WENN NUR ALLE RÄUME SO EINDEUTIG IHREN ZWECK ERFÜLLTEN...

NICOLAUS SCHAFHAUSEN: Euer Anspruch an das Publikum ist hoch: erst wer sich ausdauernd mit dem Zwiespalt: "Was soll ich sehen?" – "Wie soll ich sehen?" befasst hat, versteht die Mechanismen von Darstellung und konditionierter Wahrnehmung. Steht diese didaktische Produktionsweise nicht im Widerspruch zum Kunstverständnis der letzten Jahre? Vom Betrachter wird doch heute mehr Eigenleistung und freie Interpretation erwartet?
Die Dramaturgien in Euren Filmen irritieren, da die Wahrnehmung stets auf ordnende Zusammenhänge sinnt. Das heißt, Ihr zwingt die Betrachter - ich möchte sagen - in ein Korsett der beschränkten Wahrnehmungsmöglichkeiten. Ist die Erziehung des Betrachters notwendig? "Darf" er nur das denken, was Ihr ihm gebt?

JEROEN DE RIJKE/WILLEM DE ROOIJ: Zuerst entscheiden wir über die Bedeutung eines Werkes, dann wählen wir seine Form, und wenn wir zuerst über die Form entscheiden, dann ist das nur deshalb so, weil wir ihre Bedeutung mögen. Vor allem aber mögen wir die Form aufgrund ihrer Schönheit.
Wir mögen nun mal Ordnung. Wir haben ein Gefühl größtmöglicher intellektueller und spiritueller Freiheit, wenn wir z.B. ein Werk von Donald Judd oder Jan Vermeer oder Stanley Brouwn betrachten. Dies sind Künstler, die sowohl formal als auch inhaltlich nach einem genau definierten Raster arbeiten. Doch zwischen den Linien dieses Rasters gibt es sehr viel Freiraum... Wir sind keine Expressionisten, wir kalkulieren jeden Schritt sehr genau und hoffen, dass die Lücken in unserem Raster den Betrachtern genug Freiraum für ihre Interpretation bieten.

Obwohl unsere Arbeiten nicht - wie offensichtlich viele Leute denken - für die Meditation konzipiert sind, setzen sie sich mit dieser Thematik auseinander. Bei der Zen-Meditation dient ein Kodex strikter Verhaltensregeln, der bis zu einem Grad des physischen Schmerzes reicht, in letzter Instanz dazu, geistigen Freiraum zu schaffen.

Wir genießen es, in einem Museum zu stehen und ein Gemälde zu betrachten. Wir mögen die konventionellen Ausstellungs- und Betrachtungsweisen einer 2D-Arbeit. Der Vorgang des Beobachtens ist uns wichtig, und die Art und Weise, in der Rezipient und Projektion zueinander positioniert sind, ist selbst Bestandteil der Installation. Innerhalb eines von uns gesetzten Rahmens gibt es zahlreiche Interpretationsmöglichkeiten. Wir ziehen es allerdings vor, unsere Werke in einem Raum zu zeigen, der nur auf eine Funktion ausgerichtet ist: die Konfrontation mit und gegebenenfalls die Kontemplation eines Kunstwerkes. Wenn nur alle Räume so eindeutig ihren Zweck erfüllten...

Es gibt genug Spielraum für "Eigenleistung" in unserer Arbeit, innerhalb der Grenzen, die wir hierfür setzen. Interaktivität interessiert uns nicht. Für uns ist ein Kunstwerk ein Kunstwerk und ein Betrachter ein Betrachter. Wir empfinden die Distanz, die über diese Konstruktion geschaffen wird, als sehr angenehm.

Natürlich haben wir davon gehört, dass freie Interpretation den Schlüssel zur Kunst der 90er liefern soll. Weshalb dieser Wunsch geäußert wird, haben wir jedoch nie ganz verstanden. Warum sollte es einem Betrachter plötzlich nicht mehr genügen, einfach etwas anzuschauen? Unserer Meinung nach stellt das Anschauen unserer Werke bereits eine Eigenleistung des Betrachters dar.

Ein anderes weit verbreitetes Wort ist "großzügig". Offensichtlich meint man damit, dass ein Künstler geben und geben und geben und dafür sorgen soll, dass das Publikum zufrieden ist, zufrieden mit sich selbst und mit seinen Interpretationen. Der Künstler sollte hierbei witzig, smart und freundlich sein. Aber ein Künstler ist kein Sozialarbeiter, auch kein Event Makler, und ein Kunstwerk muss auch nicht nett aussehen. Es ist ganz in Ordnung, wenn der Betrachter etwas zu tun hat.

Die formalen Raster, mit denen wir innerhalb und außerhalb des Bildes arbeiten, sind, wie jedes Raster, ziemlich abstrakt. Anscheinend finden viele junge Künstler abstrakte Kunst "zu elitär" und sind der Meinung, die Kunst sollte so bald wie möglich auf Institutionen verzichten können und damit für ein breiteres Publikum zugänglich werden. Unser Standpunkt ist diesem diametral entgegengesetzt. Wir stören uns nicht daran, dass Kunst elitär ist, im Gegenteil, wir finden es klasse, dass sie elitär ist. Wir wollen kein Massenprodukt kreieren, wir sind nicht demokratisch.

Das soll natürlich nicht heißen, wir seien immer glücklich über das Publikum, das sich für unsere Kunst interessiert. Vielleicht träumt jeder Künstler von einem idealen Publikum. Nicht jeder, der zufällig über genug Zeit und Geld verfügt, um in eine Bücherei oder ein Museum gehen zu können, ist ein intelligenter Betrachter. Deshalb ist es wichtig, dass Museen und Galerien für Menschen aus verschiedenen sozialen Schichten zugänglich sind.

Jeder Künstler trifft Entscheidungen in seiner Arbeit. Es wäre seltsam anzunehmen, dass eine bestimmte Entscheidung dem Betrachter wesentlich bedeutsamer erscheint als eine andere. Vermutlich interpretiert jeder Betrachter unter einem anderen Gesichtspunkt. Wir persönlich fühlen uns immer ziemlich genötigt, wenn ein Künstler uns durch seine Arbeit den Eindruck vermitteln möchte: "Entscheidet Euch nach Gutdünken, wie Ihr meine Arbeit verstehen wollt!" Das ist so, als würde man einen Fremden treffen, der, nachdem er einem sein ganzes Leben erzählt hat, schließlich sagt: "Mensch, jetzt habe ja nur ich die ganze Zeit geredet. Nun erzählen Sie doch auch mal was über sich!" Was soll man darauf sagen? Für eine Antwort würde man hier eine spezifischere Frage benötigen.

Wir machen uns keine Gedanken über ein potenzielles Zielpublikum, wenn wir ein Werk realisieren. Vielleicht sind wir gar nicht so sehr daran interessiert herauszufinden, was das Publikum denkt.

N. SCH.: Mich hat vor allem Euer letzter Film *Of Three Men* mit seiner Beschäftigung mit einem "kulturellen Ort" beeindruckt, der einen spezifischen "konkreten Ort" thematisiert. Und zwar, weil er die zunehmende Homogenisierung, die die sogenannte "kulturelle Globalisierung" mit sich zu bringen scheint, grundsätzlich nicht in Frage stellt.

Was hat Euch dazu gebracht, eine neo-romanische Kirche in Amsterdam, die heute als Moschee genutzt wird, zum Inhalt Eures Filmes zu machen?

D. RI./D. RO.: Wir hatten nach einer Moschee gesucht. In Istanbul hatten wir einige wirklich schöne Moscheen gesehen und waren beeindruckt von deren Proportionen. Wir sind an unseren christlichen Altar gewöhnt, der am Ende eines rechteckigen, tunnelartigen Raumes steht. Eine Moschee ist quadratisch und wirkt geräumiger, nicht zuletzt deshalb, weil keine Bänke darin stehen. Zum einen ist dort Raum und Licht, zum anderen muss man nicht all diese nutzlosen und hässlichen Dinge anschauen, die einen im alltäglichen Leben umgeben. Sich beim Beten in eine bestimmte Richtung zu wenden (nach Osten hin), ruft ein wesentlich stärkeres Gefühl hervor als das Anbeten eines zentral fokussierten Punktes, wie z.B. des Kreuzes. Auch die Verweigerung des Bildes gefiel uns und die Tatsache, dass die gesamte Dekoration einer Moschee abstrakt sein sollte und die sich wiederholenden abstrakten Schemata dazu gedacht sind, beim Betrachter den Gedanken an Gott hervorzurufen. In unserer Phantasie entstand eine Mischung aus der Moschee und dem "white cube" mit seinen modernen Gemälden dekoriert, weil wir Spaß daran hatten, über leere weiße Räume mit abstrakten Oberflächen zu reflektieren. Dies änderte sich natürlich sofort, als wir die Fatih Moschee entdeckt hatten, denn sie sah nicht wie ein "white cube" aus, sondern eher wie ein Gemälde von Saenredam, *De St. Odolphuskerk te Assendelft*, das uns sehr gut gefällt.

Saenredams Bilder versuchen, den göttlichen Geist mittels Befolgung strikter perspektivischer Regeln heraufzubeschwören. Menschliche Figuren scheinen nur den Zweck zu erfüllen, den sie umgebenden umfangreichen, unerschütterlichen Raum hervorzuheben.

Wir waren glücklich darüber, eine Moschee gefunden zu haben, die einmal als christliche Kirche gedient hatte, obwohl das sowohl unsere Pläne als auch den Inhalt des Films drastisch modifizierte.

N. SCH.: Soll mit den Wahrnehmungsmöglichkeiten zweier konkurrierender Gesellschaftsmodelle die Unmöglichkeit der Vereinbarkeit von geografischen Kontexten aufgezeigt werden?

D. RI./D. RO.: Kulturen sind stark. In der Regel halten die Menschen über lange Zeiträume hinweg an ihnen fest. Das kann man deutlich am Beispiel der surinamesischen Bevölkerung Amsterdams erkennen. In Surinam hatten verschiedene ethnische Gruppen über Jahrhunderte hinweg zusammen gelebt: südamerikanische Indianer (Ureinwohner), Kreolen (die im 17. Jahrhundert durch holländische Kolonialherren auf Sklavenschiffen aus Ghana abtransportiert worden waren), Chinesen, Javanesen (die von den Holländern aus ihrer anderen Kolonie, Indonesien, überführt worden waren) und Hindustaner (die als Vertragsarbeiter aus Indien überführt worden waren) und natürlich die Holländer selbst. Nach Surinams Unabhängigkeit 1975 entschieden sich zahlreiche Einwohner für ein Leben in Holland. Die Hindustaner und die Inder in Amsterdam kaufen in den gleichen Läden ihre Nahrungsmittel ein und leihen in den gleichen Videotheken *Bollywood*-Filme aus. Eine Untersuchung ergab unlängst, dass es auch in der kreolischen und ghanesischen Bevölkerung Amsterdams viele gemeinsame Bräuche gibt.

Offenbar sind die Menschen so flexibel, dass sie immer, auch unter extremen Umständen sowie nach drastischen Änderungen in ihrer kulturellen und geografischen Umgebung, Möglichkeiten zur

Ausübung ihrer Bräuche und Rituale finden. Vielleicht macht unser Film deutlich, dass diese Prozesse zu ungewöhnlichen Hybrid-Resultaten führen können. Wir sehen diese Ergebnisse überall. Was der Film nicht zeigt, ist das Alltagsleben Amsterdams: die Menschen haben zu einer mehr oder weniger friedlichen Ko-Existenz gefunden (obwohl in der letzten Zeit vor allem marokkanische Teenager aufbegehren, weil sie mit ihrer Situation sehr unzufrieden sind). Doch nur in sehr seltenen Fällen funktioniert die wechselseitige Integration von Holländern und den restlichen 50 Prozent der Bevölkerung in dieser Stadt. Eines der größten Probleme, dem sich die Stadt innerhalb der nächsten 10 Jahre gegenübersehen wird, ist die Zunahme bei der Herausbildung von schwarzen Schulen, in denen die Schüler innerhalb kürzester Zeit Defizite beim Erlernen der holländischen Sprache aufweisen; das hat fatale Folgen für ihre Zukunft.

N. SCH.: Soll der Film also auch bedeuten, dass wir uns zwar alle in einem geografischen Kontext aufhalten können, das Leben dadurch aber nur noch in Chatrooms möglich wird?

D. RI./D. RO.: Es erscheint doch ganz normal, dass man auch in einem fremden Land zuerst in den eigenen Chatroom geht. Wir haben ein halbes Jahr in Bombay und Umgebung gelebt und lernten dort nur Filmproduzenten kennen. Nur weil man in ein anderes Land übersiedelt, muss man nicht plötzlich Kontakt mit Klempnern und Kuhhirten knüpfen. Das macht man zu Hause schließlich auch nicht.
Natürlich kann man Kontakt zu Leuten aus anderen Chatrooms herstellen, aber das bedingt immer jede Menge Übersetzungsprobleme (selbst wenn man die gleiche Sprache spricht), Energie und Zeit und, ganz offen gesagt, glauben wir, dass die wenigsten Leute bereit sind, so viel Mühe auf sich zu nehmen. Die Menschen haben schon immer in Chatrooms gelebt. Vielleicht ist es für einige Leute ein Problem, dass derzeit die verschiedenen Chatrooms einerseits

vielfältiger, andererseits aber auch kleiner werden.

Vielleicht verbringen ja die Leute, die allzu sehr um die Globalisierung besorgt sind, zuviel Zeit in ihrem eigenen sozialen Zirkel, in ihrem eigenen Chatroom, unabhängig davon, in welchem Erdteil sich dieser befinden mag. Würde einer von ihnen einmal einen Monat mit einer Familie verbringen, die entweder nur über die Hälfte oder aber das Doppelte des eigenen Einkommens verfügt oder sehr religiös lebt (wobei es keinen Unterschied macht, um welche Religion es sich hierbei handelt), dann würde er, selbst wenn diese Familie in seiner eigenen Stadt lebte, die Unterschiede wesentlich deutlicher spüren.

Unserer Meinung nach rührt dieses ganze Globalisierungstrauma nur daher, dass die Leute zu viele Flughäfen zu Gesicht bekommen, und selbst dort können wir noch viele Unterschiede entdecken.

Die Tatsache, dass die Ähnlichkeiten verschiedener Orte für den Betrachter heute stärker zutage treten, bedeutet nicht, dass alle Unterschiede verschwunden sind. Sie verlagern sich nur wo anders hin. Wahrscheinlich werden sie subtiler. Wir interessieren uns für subtile Unterschiede, für Nuancen.

Wir reisten nach Grönland, um *I'm Coming Home in Forty Days* zu drehen. Auf den ersten Blick wirkt das Land ziemlich karg: es scheint nur aus Fels, Moos, Himmel, Wasser und Eis zu bestehen. Doch bei genauerer Betrachtung des Mooses entdeckt man Millionen verschiedener Moosarten, und auch das Eis sieht niemals gleich aus, weil es das Wasser spiegelt; das Wasser wiederum spiegelt den Himmel. Ein schwimmender Eisberg kann an einem neuen Ort völlig fremd wirken. All diese Nuancen kann man nur wahrnehmen, wenn man Zeit investiert.

Alles wird subtiler, detaillierter und spezialisierter. Ein alter Hit wird neu abgemischt und wird wieder zu einem Hit. Danach wird sein

Remix neu abgemischt. Hierbei werden die Ähnlichkeiten - und damit auch die Unterschiede - im Vergleich zum vorherigen Mix betont. Jedoch sollte ein guter Remix auch einen guten Beat haben. Wenn der inzwischen nicht mehr "in" ist, wird er dem heutigen Geschmack angepasst. Natürlich könnte man sagen, dass alle Songs gleich klingen und dass der Remix wie das Original klingt. Aber das zu behaupten wäre absolut komisch, weil es sich doch um zwei verschiedene Dinge handelt! Selbst wenn der Remix schlecht ist. In letzter Instanz wird derjenige, der den Remix macht, zum Star, d.h. derjenige, der lediglich das existierende Material neu organisiert, es neu kombiniert. In der Kunstszene ist dies der Kurator.

Vielleicht gibt es heute sogar mehr Unterschiede als früher, aber sie sind unerheblicher. Wenn die Unterschiede geringer werden oder sich verlagern, muss man eben wieder nach ihnen suchen. Zu leugnen, dass sie existieren, wäre zu einfach.
Es wäre wohl kalt und zynisch anzunehmen, dass sich die Unterschiede alle nivellieren. Eine solche Annahme zeigt nur, dass jemand nicht genau hinsehen kann oder zu faul dazu ist.

N. SCH.: Zeigt *Of Three Men* nicht auch, dass es unmöglich ist, unterschiedliche gesellschaftliche Lebensmodelle wertfrei von den Autoren und Rezipienten zu trennen? Das heißt, bedeutet die Aussage des Films nicht, dass das Kommunikationsproblem der Gegenwart die unterschiedlichen Kommunikationsmodelle selbst sind?

D. RI./D. RO.: Ja, viele der Schwierigkeiten, mit denen die Menschen in multikulturellen Gesellschaften wie Amsterdam konfrontiert sind, sind auf große Übersetzungs- und Kommunikationsprobleme zurückzuführen. Aber das ist dem Film nicht zu entnehmen. Der Film handelt u.a. von zwei Kulturen, die unvorhergesehen an einem bestimmten Ort aufeinandertreffen und von dem Schönen und Ungewöhnlichen dieser Begegnung und von den architektonischen

Extravaganzen, die daraus resultieren.

N. SCH.: Die Handlungsorte Eurer Filme stehen stets außerhalb alltäglicher Lebensumfelder für einen westlich sozialisierten Menschen. Die gewählten Orte entziehen sich also dem Alltag und sind dadurch per se künstlich.
Wollt Ihr aufklären, wie exotisch doch alles sein kann? Ist diese Haltung nicht zu moralisierend?

D. RI./D. RO.: Das hängt davon ab, was man unter "exotisch" versteht. Wenn man Exotik mit Moral verbindet, impliziert man eine kolonialistische Lesart des Wortes, die in enger Verbindung mit Schuldbewusstsein steht. Das interessiert uns aber nicht. Wir wollen nicht politisch korrekt sein. Was bedeutet in diesem Zusammen-hang überhaupt "korrekt"? Keines unserer Werke beansprucht für sich Moral.
Würden wir nur weiße Schauspieler engagieren, hieße es, unsere Arbeit handele davon, was es bedeutet, weiß zu sein. Oder würden wir nur in den Niederlanden drehen, würde man sagen, unsere Arbeit setzt sich mit der holländischen Wesensart auseinander etc. Unsere Art, über Menschen oder Orte zu reflektieren, hat damit aber rein gar nichts zu tun.

Wir haben unterschiedliche und manchmal ambivalente Blickwinkel, wenn es um Exotik geht. Als wir außerhalb unserer alltäglichen Umgebung filmten, versuchten wir, Bilder zu machen, die aussahen, als hätte man sie überall auf der Welt aufnehmen können. Wir wollten keinen Film über Indien drehen, aus dem Grund mussten wird erst dorthin gehen, um das klarzustellen.
Als wir in den Niederlanden filmten, wählten wir exotische, aber spezifisch holländische Plätze: den Botanischen Garten Amsterdams (eine Vorstellung von tropischen Landschaften, wie man sie im 19. Jahrhundert hatte) und den Schmetterlingsgarten des Emmener

Zoos (eine holländische Version des Regenwaldes aus den 1970ern). Dieser Botanische Garten ist genauso holländisch wie ein Kanal, weil er niederländischem Gedankengut entstammt.
Uns gefällt es, dass diese Gärten Vorstellungen abbilden, sie wirken fast wie Gemälde.

Eine schöne Definition des Exotischen hat Peter Mason in seinem Buch *Infelicities* aufgestellt. Er beschreibt das exotische Objekt als Produkt eines Vorgangs, bei dem eine Kultur durch eine andere transportiert, dekontextualisiert und neuinterpretiert wird. Das ist ein Prozess der "Exotisierung". "Das Exotische ist nie zu Hause", bemerkt er. Es wird von der Kultur, in die es transportiert wird, missverstanden, dagegen existiert es an seinem Ursprungsort gar nicht als solches, weil die Menschen es nicht als exotisch ansehen. Uns gefällt diese Vorstellung vom Exotischen als Leerstelle, als etwas Fließendes, das nirgendwo hingehört.

Auf jeden Fall differenzieren wir ganz genau zwischen dem Exotischen und dem Artifiziellen.

Unsere Bilder entspringen nicht dem Alltagsleben, sondern Phantasien oder anderen Bildern. Sobald wir ein Bild im Kopf haben, suchen wir nach einem Ort, der so aussieht wie der in unserer Phantasie. Dieser Ort ist für irgendjemanden oder -etwas eine Alltagsrealität. Bisher haben wir noch nie selbst die Szenarien für einen Film konstruiert. Wir verändern bestimmte Kleinigkeiten an einem Ort, aber nicht sehr viel. Wir machen jedoch nie Dokumentarfilme.
In diesem Sinne sind wir ganz traditionell: für uns ist Kunst Darstellung und somit immer ein geistiges Konstrukt.
Außerdem verstehen wir auch gar nicht, warum heutzutage so viel darüber diskutiert wird, ob Kunst nun etwas Künstliches ist oder nicht. Unserer Meinung nach war Kunst immer schon künstlich. Wir dachten immer, genau das mache ihr Wesen aus.

Kunst ist künstlich, und wir finden das gut.

Wir halten es für problematisch, wenn Künstler vorgeben, ihre Kunst sei Realität, wie all die Fotografen, die stilisierte Fotos machen.

Diese ganze Bewegung, die die Grenzen zwischen Fälschung und Realität untersucht, erscheint uns ziemlich uninteressant und trivial. Was uns angeht, hat es nie einen Zweifel hinsichtlich des Realen und des Künstlichen gegeben. Was nicht real ist, wird niemals wahr sein, auch wenn wir nicht wissen, dass es nicht real ist.

N. SCH.: Eure Arbeiten sind auch zutiefst romantisch. Sie resultieren aus der Auseinandersetzung mit Vergangenem – zeigen aber keine Wege auf, was daraus zu machen ist oder was sein könnte.

Ist das utopische Moment in aktueller Kunstproduktion überhaupt noch möglich?

D. RI./D. RO.: Es wäre ziemlich bitter, wenn man nicht mehr in Utopien denken könnte. Unserer Meinung nach beschäftigt sich Kunst mit "erhabenen" Momenten, Träumen, Phantasien und Prophezeihungen.

Je mehr Emotionen ein Kunstwerk in einem Betrachter hervorrufen kann, desto besser ist es. Wir fänden es toll, ein Werk zu kreieren, das alle Leute zu Tränen rührt.

Aber wir sind uns nicht so sicher, ob sich unser Werk mit Utopien auseinandersetzt. Wir sehen unsere Arbeiten mehr als die Visualisierung einer Annahme über eine bestimmte Realität. Wir wollen einen Film machen, ein Film über "alles". Wann wir ihn machen werden, wissen wir jetzt noch nicht. In letzter Zeit haben wir viele epische Filme angeschaut: *Lawrence von Arabien*, *Barry Lyndon*.

Das Epische ist charakteristisch für Hollywoodproduktionen.

Wir glauben nicht, dass es möglich ist, sei es in der Vergangenheit oder heutzutage, Kunst zu kreieren, ohne an Utopien zu glauben.

Unseres Erachtens hat jeder Künstler Visionen von erhabener Schönheit. Wir alle wollen uns selbst übertreffen, um das ultimative

Kunstwerk zu erschaffen, und wir alle arbeiten daran, den Menschen auch noch nach unserem Tode in der Erinnerung zu bleiben.

Wir sind ferner der Ansicht, dass alle Künstler, die nicht mit dieser Geisteshaltung an ihre Arbeit herangehen, zu nichts anderem in der Lage sind, als ihre eigene Identitätskrise zu kommentieren.

N. SCH.: Ihr sagt zwar - und zeigt es ja auch - dass Zeit ein essenziell wichtiger Bestandteil Eurer Arbeiten ist.
Aber warum bewegt Ihr Euch dann nicht in der Gegenwart?

D. RI./D. RO.: Ja, wir denken, dass man für die Betrachtung eines schönen Bildes Zeit braucht. Wir sind gewissermaßen auf einer Mission mit dem Ziel, Bilder, die wir erkannt haben, in unseren Köpfen zu konservieren. Bilder werden wie Müll behandelt. Man schaut sie nicht einmal an. Aus diesem Grund sind wir nicht so sehr daran interessiert, jede Woche ein neues Bild zu kreieren. Man würde es nicht einmal bemerken, außerdem arbeiten wir nicht so schnell. Vermutlich kann das kein Künstler.

Es ist unsere Aufgabe, die von uns produzierten Bilder vor allzu großer Abnutzung zu bewahren und unser Publikum vor der visuellen Überfrachtung zu schützen, die es selbst zu verantworten hat.

Letzte Woche bat uns ein Grafiker, ihm einige Bilder für einen Artikel in einer holländischen Kunstzeitschrift zur Verfügung zu stellen. Als wir ihm drei Fotos gaben, lachte er uns ins Gesicht und meinte: "Nur drei?" Dann, als er die Dias anschaute, indem er sie zwei Sekunden lang gegen das Deckenlicht hielt, fügte er hinzu: "Das ist ja gar kein Bild." Nur eins von drei Fotos ließ er als Bild gelten. Es ist ein Dia mit einem spärlich bekleideten jungen Mädchen mit großen Titten. Die Designer von *Nu Magazine* wollten "zehn oder mehr Bilder, damit eine Auswahl möglich ist". Als wir nur zwei sandten, um die Auswahloption zu verringern, entschlossen sie sich, eines davon als Farbhintergrund für den (exzellenten)

Text zu verwenden. Tatsächlich haben wir nicht einmal zehn Bilder zuhause herumliegen, schließlich sind wir keine Bilderfabrik.

Als wir noch jung waren, gab es in Holland ein Modemagazin namens *Avenue*. *Avenue* betonte seine Monopolstellung auf moderne Art: Es predigte die Wahrheit und nichts als die Wahrheit. Wenn Wina Born (*Avenues* Korrespondentin für Kulinarisches) in ihrer Kolumne gegen Basilikum wetterte, wollte niemand dabei erwischt werden, irgendetwas mit Basilikum zu würzen, da er sonst out gewesen wäre. Keiner der Leser hätte diesbezüglich je einen Zweifel gehegt. Die Autorität Wina Borns konnte nicht erschüttert werden. Es war schlicht eine Diktatur des Stils. Sehr modern und so einfach! Es war nicht nötig, eine Wahl zu treffen oder selbst eine Position zu beziehen. Das sparte Zeit und Verwirrung. Vielleicht ist es ja altmodisch, an Klarheit zu glauben, doch wir glauben daran. Mitte der 80er ließ *Avenues* guter Ruf nach und andere Magazine erschienen. Die Herausgeber hatten eine sehr postmoderne Idee: die *Avenue Box*. Diese Box würde jeden Monat unterschiedliche Zutaten und ein anderes Thema haben. Beispielsweise die Japan Box, die u.a. zwei Holzstäbchen enthielt...

Avenue machte bald darauf Bankrott. Der ehemalige Chefredakteur leitet nun das *APMagazine*, ein kostenloses monatliches Blättchen von einer relativ unbekannten holländischen Supermarktkette.

N. SCH.: Ihr wollt Eure Arbeit als Bilder betrachtet sehen. Ihr produziert Filme. Versteht Ihr Euch als Filmemacher?

D. RI./D. RO.: Wir sind Künstler und wir produzieren Filme.

N. SCH.: In *Forever and Ever* von 1995 operiert Ihr am deutlichsten mit der Theatralik des Fotoromans. Die Kameraführung impliziert eher Filmstills, die filmisch mit größter Sorgfalt aneinander arrangiert wurden. Habt Ihr Euch hier nicht in der Form vergriffen? Wäre ein

Fotoroman nicht ausreichend - oder sogar das richtigere Medium gewesen? Ist die Form nicht nur noch Koketterie?

D. RI./D. RO.: Nein, *Forever and Ever* ist mehr als nur eine Aneinanderreihung von Bildern. Zunächst einmal sind sie nicht statisch. Die Zeit ist in jedem Bild in Bewegung, und das fühlt man auch. Die unterlegten Geräusche und das Timing bewirken bei den Rezipienten Reaktionen wie Spannung, Erwartungshaltung, ein Gefühl für den Raum und Konzentration. Die Filmproduktion ähnelt in vielerlei Hinsicht der Komposition eines musikalischen Werks.

In jedem unserer Filme wollen wir eine Geschichte erzählen. Die Erzählung entsteht durch die Kombination eines Bildes mit einem bestimmten Klang und dessen Dauer. Sobald Zeit vergeht, wird damit bereits eine Geschichte erzählt. Auch wenn sich in einem Bild nichts bewegt, wird der Betrachter seine eigene Geschichte konstruieren. Die Präsentation an sich lenkt die Erwartungshaltung auf das Erzählte. Diese Antizipation ist der erste Teil der Geschichte. Schon bevor der Film beginnt, weiß man, dass er auch ein Ende haben wird. Also muss sich zwischendrin die Geschichte befinden.

N. SCH.: *Moving images* sind hip. Ihr habt an zahlreichen solcher Genre-Ausstellungen teilgenommen. Durch die Sperrigkeit Eurer "Aufbauinstruktionen" erscheint mir das allerdings als widersprüchlich. Baut Ihr nicht eher Environments oder Erlebnisräume, wo das "bewegte Bild" nur ein Zufallsprodukt ist?

D. RI./D. RO.: Wir realisieren unsere Installationen mit sehr viel Konzentration. Innerhalb eines uns zugewiesenen oder selbst gewählten Raumes versuchen wir, eine atmosphärische Mischung aus Kino und Ausstellungsfläche zu schaffen. Die von uns produzierten Filme haben einen spezifischen Anfang und ein spezifisches Ende und sollten in ihrer Gesamtheit rezipiert werden.

Zum Beispiel kann ein Film innerhalb einer Stunde zweimal angesehen werden. Eine Zeitanzeige an der Wand informiert den Betrachter über die Dauer des Films. Es gibt Bänke für die Zuschauer. Der Raum ist sauber, leer und liegt im Halbdunkel, so dass seine Dimensionen noch wahrgenommen werden können. Alle Störfaktoren wie Leuchtschilder, Spiegelungen oder Lärm werden weitestgehend reduziert. Mit besonderer Sorgfalt wird berücksichtigt, was man auf der Bank sitzend aus den Augenwinkeln wahrnehmen kann. Der Projektor befindet sich in einer schalldichten Kiste. Diese Kiste ist, wie alles andere, was wir in diesem Raum aufstellen (Lautsprecher, Bänke), rein funktional. Wie diese Dinge im Raum plaziert werden, ist wichtig, weil der Raum während der Ausstellung in der Regel nicht von dem Film ausgefüllt wird. Wir verstehen diesen Raum als eine minimale Skulptur.

Daher sind diese Räume mehr als nur Erlebnisräume, sie wurden speziell für unsere Filme entwickelt und sollen auch ohne die Filmprojektion wirken. Leere ist für unsere Filme genauso wichtig wie für die von uns gestalteten Räume, in denen sie gezeigt werden. Darüber hinaus haben wir bedacht, dass ein Publikum in verschiedenster Hinsicht konditioniert ist, und versuchen daher, eine Raumsituation zu schaffen, die es den Zuschauern erlaubt, sich auf einen Film zu konzentrieren, ohne sich dabei unwohl zu fühlen. Der Kontext, in dem eine Arbeit gezeigt wird, beeinflusst das Ausstellungsobjekt und seine Rezeption durch den Betrachter, so dass man den Eindruck gewinnt, die Wirkung des Werkes gehe weit über seinen Rahmen hinaus. Würden wir Gemälde herstellen, dann würden wir genau das Gleiche tun.

N. SCH.: Ihr habt Euch schon öfter dahingehend geäußert, dass vor allem Sound bei Ausstellungen vernachlässigt oder als unwichtig von Ausstellungsmachern betrachtet wird.
Wie erklärt Ihr Euch diese Nachlässigkeiten? Oder handelt es sich um grundsätzliche Kommunikationsprobleme bei der Öffentlich-

machung von Kunst zwischen Produzent und Ausstellungsort? Legt Ihr aus diesem Grund so viel Wert auf strikte Beachtung Eurer Ausstellungs-/Aufbauinszenierungen?

D. RI./D. RO.: In den meisten Gruppenausstellungen werden Künstler, die - wie wir - Sound produzieren, gebeten, die Soundtracks zu ihren Werken mit denen von anderen an der Ausstellung teilnehmenden Künstlern zur Herstellung einer Gesamtkomposition mischen zu lassen. Diese Frage wird im allgemeinen ca. eine Stunde vor der Eröffnung entschieden, und die Künstler sollen dann zusammenkommen, um sich "miteinander abzustimmen". Das wirklich Demütigende daran ist, dass man mit seinen Künstlerkollegen regelrecht verhandeln muss. Beide Seiten wissen in diesem Moment, dass mal wieder ein Kompromiss gezeigt werden wird. In der Regel werden aus Gründen der Geldknappheit, der Ignoranz und "weil die Kontinuität der Ausstellung nicht beeinträchtigt werden soll" nicht die erforderlichen Maßnahmen getroffen, um diese schmerzhaften Momente und die sinnlose Amputation der Kunstwerke zu verhindern. Aber was macht Kontinuität überhaupt für einen Sinn in einer Ausstellung, in der nur die Hälfte eines jeden Werkes erfasst werden kann?

Das Kuratieren basiert scheinbar meistens auf dem Bild oder dem Inhalt, manchmal sogar auf beiden. Doch wenn die Kuratoren darauf insistieren, aus den Sounds zu den verschiedenen Werken ihre eignen Kompositionen zu machen, sollten sie vielleicht damit anfangen, die Soundtracks zu sammeln.

Natürlich ist es verrückt und dumm zu denken, dass der eine Teil eines Kunstwerkes weniger Aufmerksamkeit benötige als irgendein anderer. Oder dass ein Aspekt weniger wichtig sei als ein anderer. Das ist, als würde man zwei Skulpturen übereinandergestapelt ausstellen. Man kann allerdings den Kurator nicht dafür verantwortlich machen, dass er nicht weiß, wie ein bestimmtes Kunstwerk ausgestellt werden sollte. Das muss der Künstler ihm/ihr sagen. Es gibt auch Künstler, denen es nichts ausmacht, wenn ihr Sound mit dem anderer Künstler gemischt wird. Manche finden das sogar gut. Aber wenn alle, die das nicht wollen, weiterhin ungenügende Bedingungen bei der Zurschaustellung ihrer Werke akzeptieren, wird sich nichts ändern.

N. SCH.: Wie haltet Ihr es dann überhaupt mit der kuratorischen Autorenschaft?

D. RI./D. RO.: Es ist irgendwie seltsam, dass viele der Starkuratoren durch ihre thematischen Gruppenausstellungen berühmt werden. Gerade diese Gruppenausstellungen sind für Künstler häufig problematisch. Bei der Produktion unserer Arbeiten denken wir nicht darüber nach, wie sie im Kontext einer Gruppenausstellung wirken könnten.

Die kuratorische Autorenschaft ist vielleicht einer der Gründe dafür, dass so viele Künstler ihre Arbeiten in den Gesamtraum ausdehnen, wie dies derzeit der Fall ist. Genau deshalb brauchen viele von uns abgetrennte Räume, Kabinen oder Zellen: um sich vor dem Horror des Kuratiert-Werdens zu schützen.
Glücklicherweise werden die meisten intelligenten Leute, wenn ein kuratorisches Konzept missrät, höchstens darüber lachen und versuchen, die Kunst unter dem Müll zu entdecken. Aber das macht die Sache auch nicht besser.

Natürlich gibt es auch wirklich hervorragende Kuratoren. Sie haben eine originelle Vision. Es war z.B. phantastisch, mit Harm Lux zu arbeiten. Er schaffte es tatsächlich, etwas an einer Arbeit zu ergänzen und sie damit zu verbessern, auch war er sehr smart und engagiert. Vielleicht ist das Hauptproblem bei der kuratorischen Autorenschaft, dass wir heute, nach ihrer Erfindung, nicht mehr den Schritt zurück vollziehen können. Niemals mehr werden wir zwei Kunstwerke anschauen können, ohne darüber zu reflektieren, warum sie nebeneinander gestellt wurden und von wem...

Eine neue Entwicklung bei der kuratorischen Selbstaffirmation ist der Wunsch, selbst etwas zu produzieren. In zunehmendem Maße hört man die Kritik der Kuratoren an ihren Kollegen, weil diese angeblich Ausstellungen mit protzigen Themenstellungen und peinlichen Titeln organisierten. Der neue Kurator tut so etwas natürlich nicht, aber er kann gar nicht darauf warten, stolz zu verkünden: "Oh, Sie kennen die Arbeit von So und So?" – "Ja, die habe ich produziert" oder: "Ich habe diese Arbeit zuerst gezeigt".
Die Kuratoren haben innerhalb kurzer Zeit eine Entwicklung durchgemacht von organisierenden Bürokraten, die im Schatten der Kontext-Macher thematischer Gruppenausstellungen agierten, hin zu Erfindern und Produzenten ("Ich habe diese Arbeit fast noch vor dem Künstler entdeckt und eine Stunde später schon ausgestellt.").

Natürlich ist es heutzutage toll und auch absolut unerlässlich, dass die Ausstellungsmacher in kompliziertere, teurere und zeitaufwendige Produktionen involviert werden. Aber wenn dies nur zu einem weiteren Mittel dafür wird, die bei sich selbst vermutete Großzügigkeit zur Schau stellen zu wollen, ist es einem Künstler unter Umständen lieber, das hässliche Logo eines anonymen Sponsors in elaboriertem Druck auf ihrer Arbeit zu sehen. Falsche Integrität macht ein Kunstwerk nicht besser.

VEIT LOERS
BEOBACHTUNGEN ZU DE RIJKE/DE ROOIJS *OF THREE MEN*

Der letzte Film der beiden Künstler Jeroen de Rijke und Willem
de Rooij *Of three men* ist ihr größter: 35 mm bei 10 Minuten Laufzeit.
Was einen erwartet, ist ein in der Relation aufwendiges Format, ein
sorgsames Arrangement und ein Mise-en-Scène mit dem Anspruch
eines Kinofilms im Museum; ein leerer dunkler Raum, in dem
sich eine Wand öffnet und den Blick in ein Kircheninterieur freigibt.
Die Arbeit besteht zu einem guten Stück aus Inszenierung.
Nicht nur, was die Vorgaben der Aufführung betrifft, sondern auch
den Inhalt des Films. Der Blick in ein Kircheninneres wird inszeniert,
aber auf der Bühne gibt es keine Handlung. Der Blick trifft nicht
gerade ins Leere, doch ist die unbewegte Einstellung der Kamera
deren allegorischer Ort. Vielleicht ist es auch die Beziehung des
Betrachters zum Kino. Oder es sind die Prolegomena der Filmvor-
führung und des verdunkelten Raumes: Das, was im Kino normalerweise im wörtlichen Sinne der Bedeutung abläuft, erklärt sich hier
zur Hauptsache. Aber es ist auch mehr als das. Wesentlich sind die
zehn Minuten Film, sind das auf die Wand projizierte Kircheninterieur
einer Amsterdamer Kirche.
Die Umstände der Realisierung des Films sind nicht das Entscheidende,
aber sie helfen beim Einstieg. Die Kirche ist kein mittelalterliches
Gebäude, sondern entstammt den frühen zwanziger Jahren.
Spätester Historismus und schon Teil der Moderne. Eine Gotik aus
Flächen, Linien und Raumhaftigkeit. Es überkommt einen das Gefühl
von Schwerelosigkeit, ein Zustand, den gleichzeitig die kubistischen
Kirchenbilder von Delaunay und Feininger vermitteln. Ein anderes
Moment ist die Leere der Kirche. Sie wurde zur Moschee umgewandelt
und ihr Eingang nach hinten verlegt. Sie kann deshalb auch auf das
Kirchengestühl verzichten, das sonst die Kirchenschiffe verstellt.
Mit seinen Kronleuchtern tritt das Gotteshaus in der Reinheit auf, die
schon die Romantik dazu verführte, barock ausgestattete gotische
Kathedralen in ihre Ursubstanz "zurückzuführen", um einer verloren
geglaubten Raumfiktion wieder teilhaftig zu werden.
Die Größe des Filmbildes und die Farbnuancen erklären, warum

de Rijke/de Rooij das Medium des Films und zwar eines 35 mm Films verwendeten. Video-Installationen erfahren heute mit Hilfe des Beamers ihre Wirkung durch ihre Größendimension. Die Formate von Barnett Newman, Mark Rothko, Clifford Still, die Volumen von Arbeiten Donald Judds, Carl Andres und Richard Serras, die Größe der Cibachrome von Fotografen seit den achtziger Jahren haben mit den Proportionen des Betrachters zu tun, damit, wie er diesen Arbeiten gegenübersteht.

In das Kircheninterieur von de Rijke/de Rooij müsste man, zumindest als potenzielle Wunschsituation, eintreten können. Das Maß an Hingabe wird größer, und der Blick ist nicht der angestrengte Guck-kastenillusionismus des Fernsehers. Das Interesse fokussiert sich nicht via Illustration einer anderen maßstablosen Welt, sondern der Blick kann entspannt in eine etwa gleich große Welt eintreten. Das gibt einem das Gefühl, man wäre selbst schon im Raum, obwohl sich dieser als Fata Morgana versperrt wie jeder andere Filmraum auch. Farblich sind es Gelb-Ocker- und Grautöne, durchdrungen von blauen Kontrasten, die den Eindruck bestimmen.

Wir sagten es schon: Der Innenraum geht eine merkwürdige Synthese von spätestem Historismus und früher Moderne ein. Ein Kirchen-interieur, das schon für den Film gemacht zu sein scheint und den mittelalterlichen malerischen Szenerien eines Fritz Lang (*Die Nibelungen*), eines Paul Wegener (*Der Golem*) und eines F. W. Murnau (*Faust, Nosferatu*) aus den zwanziger Jahren entspricht. Durch die Modellie-rung der Wände des Hauptschiffs und der Seitenschiffe entsteht ein Raumbild, das nicht nur vom Architekten so geplant ist, sondern durch eine kleine Verschiebung der Kamera aus der Mittelachse heraus von den Regisseuren noch unterstützt wird. Der Weitwinkel des Objektivs klappt den Raum auf, gibt ihm zugleich jene Geschlossenheit, die notwendig ist, um einen Ort zu definieren. Die reine Zentralperspektive hingegen schafft eine forcierte Raum-progression, die im imaginären Fluchtpunkt landet.

Für de Rijke/de Rooijs Idee des Films waren die Gemälde von Kircheninterieurs des Pieter Saenredam (1597 – 1665) aus Haarlem maßgeblich. Der Maler gilt als der bedeutendste Meister dieses Genres, das man durchaus als Kirchenporträt bezeichnen könnte. Man hat herausgefunden, dass er die Zentralperspektive nach den natürlichen Gegebenheiten der Kirchen veränderte und durch leichtes Verrücken der Zentralperspektive und Lichtführung eine neue Art von visionärem Raum schaffen konnte, dessen Lichtführung verrät, dass es um mehr als um einen von katholischen Altären befreiten protestantischen Kirchenraum ging. Im achtzehnten Jahrhundert war es der *scena per angolo*, also dem Bühnenbild mit zwei Perspektivpunkten, vorbehalten, den Raum sozusagen zu drehen und dem Betrachter ein Eck davon entgegenzuschieben. Dieser Einfall brachte größere Nähe und Wahrhaftigkeit bei größerer Distanz des Betrachters, erlebbar nicht nur in den Bühnenbildern des Barock, sondern auch in den *Carceri* Piranesis. Der Film *Of three men* ist zwar beinahe zentralperspektivisch aufgenommen. Durch seine Weitwinkelsicht und das schon als Bild angelegte Architekturkonzept der Kirche erfährt man jedoch eine erlebbare Raumfülle, die eine diskrete eigene Szenerie erhält, gleichzeitig aber isoliert.

Nun gibt es Momente, die aus der Bildhaftigkeit herausgehen und das Filmische betreffen. Zunächst ist es die Eingangsszene, wo mehrere Personen mit ihren Draperien als Vorhang fungieren, der sich dann plötzlich öffnet. Die Bewegungsregie geht von da an in eine qualitativ höhere Stufe über. Man erlebt den Stillstand in der einstigen Kirche kosmisch - wie das Ausatmen Bramahs. Die erlebbare Stille wird durch das langsame Drehen der Lüster aktiviert. Eine weitere Bewegungssequenz bilden Sonne und Wolken außerhalb, die die Lichtführung in der Kirche variieren. Schließlich sind es die fast unmerklichen, aber nicht zu übersehenden Bewegungen der Menschen, die das Bild im Bewegungsfluss erhalten. Man sieht rechts im Hintergrund des Hauptschiffes drei Männer in Gebetshaltung am

Boden hocken und sich ab und zu verbeugen. Eine kaum wahr-
nehmbare Figur links und ein später von vorne rechts hinzutretender
Mann sind ebenfalls Teile dieses lebendigen Rhythmus. Durch diese
Elemente atmet der Raum. Obwohl kaum sichtbar, sind diese
Gläubigen der äußere und innere Parameter für die Transzendenz
des Gotteshauses.

Bild, Raum und zeitliche Kontinuität ergeben sich aber auch durch
die ungeschnittene zehnminütige Kameraeinstellung. In ihr wird das
Moment der Dauer besonders anschaulich. Hinzu kommt der Filmton,
ein schwer zu definierendes permanentes Geräusch, ein Thematisieren
räumlicher Stille, das von außen eindringt und sich wie ein Schleier
über die Szene breitet. Alle diese Momente der Zeit mit dem
geräuschvollen Schweigen ergeben etwas sehr Merkwürdiges.
Die Offenbarung des Raums wird zur Dauer. Während am Anfang
des Films das Gefühl vorherrscht, man könne im gefilmten Raum
der Kirche bzw. Moschee innerlich aufgehen, lässt diese Vorstellung
bald nach. Das Zoom öffnet sich nicht weiter. Es ist filmtechnisch
alles erreicht, und der Kirchenprospekt beginnt zeitliche Dimensionen
anzunehmen. Es ist wie eine Art Warten, und der permanente
Rauschton lässt das Warten hören. Erst in einem Zustand relativer
Langeweile oder, euphemistischer gesagt, Meditation, wird man
der drei Männer gewahr, die im Halbschatten des Raumes aus der
Dämmerung auftauchen. Sie sind das Maß des Raumes, erscheinen
als Quelle seiner räumlich-ätherischen Substanz, obwohl sie gleichzeitig in ihm aufgehen. Die betenden Menschen geben dem Raum
außerdem eine historische Dimension. Im Islam sind die Gebetshal-
tungen archaischer geblieben. Man fühlt, dass man sich in einem
nicht genauer zu beschreibenden geschichtlichen Gebäude befindet.
Saenredam und seine Zeitgenossen wie Hendrick van Steenwijk d. J.
lassen in ihren Kircheninterieurs das Opfer Melchisedeks stattfinden
oder die nächtliche Befreiung Petri. Albrecht Altdorfer hat schon
hundert Jahre davor etwa in seinem Sebastiansaltar von St. Florian

die Handwaschung des Pilatus in eine gotische Kirche verlegt und in der berühmten Mariengeburt der Münchner Alten Pinakothek eine Hallenkirche zum Schauplatz des Geschehens gemacht.

In den Filmen de Rijke/de Rooijs geht es um Zeitgemäßes in der Form des zeitlos Gültigen: Die Apparitio des Schmetterlings und seine Vanitas-Symbolik, die Dauer der Liebe auch auf der Fotografie, das Indien von heute, das im Nirwana des Kosmos aufgeht, die Begegnung mit dem Eisberg, dessen Unnahbarkeit und Reinheit von absehbarer Dauer ist. Geschichte und Erdgeschichte werden scheu und mit gebührendem Abstand auf die Möglichkeit ihrer Bildhaftigkeit befragt. Die Filmkamera, längst gewöhnt an die distanzlose Nähe und an Indiskretion, wird zum fast neutralen Bildinstrument, das die Bilder nicht bewegen und näher bringen, sondern ihnen ihre ursprüngliche Würde und Distanz zurückgeben soll, zurückgeben an ein Publikum, das es großteils verlernt hat, die würdevolle Art der Bilder noch wahrzunehmen und, dies vor allem, weil die weltweite Aneignung von Bildern durch die Medien ganze Arbeit geleistet hat. In Holland hat vor mehr als zwanzig Jahren Bas Jan Ader etwa mit seinen Filmen *Farewell to Faraday Friends* (1971) oder *Flower Works* (1974) ähnlich stille Filme mit langen Einstellungen geschaffen, die aber weniger episch als sanft ironisch waren. Keine Frage, dass Marcel Broodthaers Filmwerk und das seines Freundes David Lamelas aus den siebziger Jahren mit in diese Kategorie gehören. Aber auch der Kinofilm hat seine Spuren im noch jungen Œuvre von de Rijke/ de Rooij hinterlassen. Stanley Kubrick z.B. lässt in seinen Filmen Innenräume wie eigene Wesen sprechen oder schweigen, d.h. man sieht in ihnen weniger Sequenzen als Bilder.

Minimal Art war nicht alleine die Form eines neuen räumlichen Kon-struktivismus, sie war vielmehr der Ausdruck einer neuen Setzung im Raum. Das Absolute, das wir uns eher anorganisch vorstellen, nahm Verbindung mit dem Raum auf oder besser gesagt mit einem Raumkasten. In den Aquarien der Museen gedeiht die Minimal Art gut.

Die Filme von de Rijke/de Rooij benötigen ebenfalls einen Raum-
kasten, um optimal in Erscheinung treten zu können. Dieser Kasten
muss dunkel sein, damit die Gesetze des Films wirksam werden
können. Der Ausstellungsraum, der heute problemlos mit Minimal
Art leben kann, kehrt seine Funktion um und wird in seiner
Leere und Dunkelheit zum idealen Ort für das Erscheinen der
gereinigten Filmbilder.
De Rijke/de Rooij assoziieren mit der gefilmten Gegenwart und der
Umwandlung vom Christlichen ins Islamische nicht nur historische
Phantasien, sondern beschwören auch die alte Einheit der drei
monotheistischen Religionen: der jüdischen, christlichen und islamischen. Rembrandts Eintauchen in die alttestamentarische Welt,
in der die bärtigen Akteure zuweilen würdevoll wie Derwische agieren,
ist nicht nur auftragsbedingt. In den asketischen Parabeln ist der
gegenwärtige Augenblick vernehmbar, eine Synthese von Spirituali-
tät, deren Entrücktheit nie zum historischen Bild wird. Die Theoso-
phische Bewegung der Helena Blavatskij vom Ende des neunzehnten
Jahrhunderts, die eine Synthese der wichtigen Weltreligionen intendierte, hatte im Amsterdam der beginnenden Moderne eine große
Bedeutung und zahlreiche Mitglieder, vor allem unter Künstlern.
Die Klarheit des Protestantismus bekam noch einmal neue Flügel.
Vielleicht ist auch dieser historische zeitgeschichtliche Hintergrund
wie eine kunsthistorische Parabel: Die in der abendländischen
Geschichte verankerte Moderne, speziell der Abstraktion und der
Minimal Art, fand im Islam, vor allem im Sufismus, ein Symbol für
ihren inhärenten Ikonoklasmus. Der Sufist muss lernen, die Welt
des Denkens, die Welt des Fühlens und die physische Welt ins
Gleichgewicht zu bringen. Zeit ist ein Attribut Gottes. Der ereignislose
Kirchenraum von *Of three men* will nicht gesehen, sondern erfahren
werden. Der Sufist sucht die Einheit des äußeren Bildes mit seinem
Inneren zu verschmelzen. Was außerhalb von einem ist, ist in Wahrheit in einem selbst. Wenn der Film von de Rijke/de Rooij aus ist,
brennt das Bild im Inneren weiter. Vielleicht kann man das Gefühl

auch mit einem Ausspruch des Franz von Assisi umschreiben:
"Was du suchst, ist das, was sucht."

VANESSA JOAN MÜLLER
NON FICTION

Die filmischen Arbeiten von Jeroen de Rijke und Willem de Rooij
sind Kino in seiner dekontextualisierten Form. Sie operieren innerhalb der dispositiven Struktur des Mediums mit seinem Reglement
der Vorführung im abgedunkelten Raum, dem genau definierten
Anfang und Ende, der latenten Verpflichtung, sich den Film in ganzer
Länge anzusehen. Andererseits situieren de Rijke/de Rooij sich
selbst und ihre Filme im Rahmen der institutionalisierten Kunst und
positionieren ihre Projektoren im klassischen "white cube"-Ambiente.
Eintritt wird an der Museumskasse gezahlt.

Diese fortgeschrittene De- und Rekontextualisierung betrifft aber
nicht nur den Rahmen dessen, was man als das apparative Erscheinen
des filmischen Bildes bezeichnen könnte, sondern auch den
Rahmen der Filmbilder selbst, die ihre Referenzen sowohl in der
Kunst finden als auch im Kino - aber eben doch eher in der Kunst.
Die Koordinaten dieses ästhetischen Bezugssystems haben sich mit
der Zeit verschoben, von der minimalistischen Abstraktion in Richtung Abstrakter Expressionismus und dann drei Jahrhunderte
zurück ins niederländische Barock. Es gibt jedoch eine Konstante in
den Filmen von de Rijke/de Rooij, die alle ästhetischen Divergenzen
überformt, und als Richtungsvektor dem gesamten Werk eine lineare
Struktur verleiht. Neben dem reduktionistischen Moment, das die
filmischen Kategorien Einstellung, Montage, Kamerabewegung einer
essentiellen Minimalisierung unterwirft, ist das der Aspekt der Zeit
als Dauer. Das klassische Raum-Zeitkontinuum, in dem der Raum
ein zu durchquerender und die Zeit eine verfließende ist, erfährt bei
de Rijke/de Rooij beinahe eine Transformation zur Bewegung im
Stillstand. Was ihre Filme liefern sind deshalb, um die substantielle
Bestimmung des Kinematografischen von Gilles Deleuze aufzunehmen, keine "Bewegungsbilder"[01], sondern bewegte Bilder, die
das Sichtbare von den Dingen und die Bewegung von der
Geschichte trennen zugunsten der Zeit als Kategorie ästhetischer

01 VGL. GILLES DELEUZE: *DAS BEWEGUNGS-BILD. KINO 1*. FRANKFURT/M. 1989.

Erfahrung. Zeit im Film meint hier die plastische Formung der fixierten, wahrnehmbaren, scheinbar verlangsamten und doch realen Gegenwart des projizierten Bildes in seiner sinnlichen Erscheinung. Als Temporalisierung der Wahrnehmung lenkt diese Zeit als wahrnehmende und wahrnehmbare zugleich den Blick auf die verschiedenen Referenzsysteme, die inneren Rahmen und Ordnungen von Sichtbarkeit. Als Bestimmung des Visuellen binden diese das Medium Film wieder ein in das System der klassischen Bildproduktionen, indem sie die Regularien und Ästhetiken des statischen Bildes einem medialen Transfer unterziehen. Diese Verortung in einem offenen Bezugssystem existenter visueller Parameter meint allerdings nicht den zitathaften Rekurs auf Bestehendes. Die konstruktive Verweigerung linearer Strukturen des Narrativen führt bei de Rijke/ de Rooij vielmehr zu einer Befragung des Visuellen als eines semiotisch codifizierten wie ästhetischen Textes, der immer wieder neu gelesen werden kann.

Chun Tian ("Frühling") von 1994 ist der erste gemeinsame Film von Jeroen de Rijke und Willem de Rooij und exponiert bereits ihr ästhetisch überformtes Interesse an einer Freilegung der Strukturen des Filmischen. Wieviel kann man weglassen, um trotzdem ein in sich geschlossenes Ganzes zu erhalten? Wieviel Distanz verträgt der Blick auf die Realität? Welche Form der Reduktion konstruiert Bilder von abstrakter Schönheit? Die Antwort darauf könnte lauten, dass es letztlich gerade die Purifikation des Narrativen und die Aufkündigung der erkennbar subjektiven Handschrift des "Auteurs" sind, die einen Film entstehen lassen, der in seinem konstruktiven Charakter das Prinzip des Schönen mit einem Gefühl von Entfremdung verbindet, das den Blick umso stärker auf die Schönheit seiner Bilder lenkt.

Chun Tian inszeniert das Exotische als minimalistische Postkartenimpression, die überall und nirgends aufgenommen sein könnte. Tatsächlich befindet sich das exotische Setting im Botanischen Garten von Amsterdam, aber so wie es ins Bild gerückt ist, erscheint es als schwer zu verortendes Konstrukt jenseits kultureller Spezifität. Sinnliche Magnolienblüten, bildfüllend, das ist das erste, was man sieht: fast ein Klischee, aber auch eine Setzung, die das Bild in eine Fotografie zu verwandeln scheint, die sich mit der Geschwindigkeit von 24 Bildern pro Sekunde wiederholt. Doch dann fährt die Kamera langsam nach links, und ein asiatisches Paar erscheint, das völlig statisch inmitten der Blütenpracht steht: ein Tableau Vivant geometrisierter Abstraktion. Die Frau rechts blickt zu dem Mann, aber dieser sieht an ihr vorbei, direkt aus dem Filmbild heraus. Die Kamera verharrt auf den beiden eine Weile, dann erscheint ein Untertitel ("You are really very beautiful"), aber niemand sagt etwas. Erst einen Augenblick später ist der Satz auf chinesisch aus dem Off zu hören. Es ist eine männliche Stimme, die spricht, aber ob sie tatsächlich zu demjenigen gehört, der zu sehen ist, bleibt genauso unklar wie die Sprache fremd. Dann folgt ein Schnitt, und die geometrische Komposition der Personen präsentiert sich in axialer Spiegelung: Jetzt ist es der Mann, der die Frau anblickt, während diese nach links aus dem Bild sieht. Nach einer Weile ist aus dem Off eine Stimme zu hören, diesmal eine weibliche. In diesem Fall ist es der Untertitel ("I love you"), der erst zeitversetzt zu sehen ist. Die Kamera zoomt langsam zurück, bis das Paar von der Blumenkulisse vollständig eingerahmt ist. Das wäre eigentlich ein schönes Schlussbild, das codiert ist, als könne es ewig so bleiben. Doch der Film endet abrupt, bevor man das Ende erwartet, unterläuft die Erfüllung seiner internen Logik und macht zunichte, was das letzte Bild suggeriert. Die Plötzlichkeit dieses Bruchs lässt das Gefühl des schönen Scheins einfach ins Nichts fallen und hinterlässt eine seltsame Leere als Abgeschnittensein vom Faden der Illusion.

Doch auch was sich in *Chun Tian* wie eine auf ihre Grundparameter reduzierte Liebesgeschichte präsentiert, erscheint trotz der unmittelbaren Schönheit der Bilder als Ausdruck größter Dissoziierung, wenn die auf Fragmente verkürzte Geschichte erklärter Zuneigung als Abfolge abstrakter Figurationen innerhalb einer standardisierten Topik inszeniert wird. So wirkt das klassische Ich-liebe-dich, das eigentlich Subjekt und Objekt sowie ein affektives Bindeglied zwischen beiden voraussetzt, reduziert auf seine lexikalische Dimension. Liebe ist hier tatsächlich nur ein Wort. Überhaupt gewinnt *Chun Tian* mit seiner Differenz zwischen dem Sprachlichen und dem Visuellen sowie den deiktischen Brüchen eine Qualität hinsichtlich der filmischen wie semantischen Dekomposition, die das Ganze in die Nähe einer abstrakten Versuchsanordnung rückt. Statt narrativer gibt es allein formale Geschlossenheit als sichtbare Einschreibung der Struktur in das Bild. Links/rechts, Schrift und Stimme, innen/außen, diese Dichotomien sind neben der Intensität der Farben und suggestiven Ästhetik der Komposition die eigentlichen organisierenden Faktoren.

So bleibt der Rahmen, der die Komposition determiniert, indirekt immer sichtbar, gerade weil die innerbildliche Blickstruktur ihn so vehement verletzt. Der Blick aus dem Rahmen heraus verlangt an sich nach einer nachfolgenden Einstellung, die das Objekt dieses Blicks zeigt, und damit die raum-zeitliche Kohärenz wahrt.

Bei de Rijke/de Rooij hingegen bleibt die Kamera die ganze Zeit auf die Personen fokussiert, während sie sich mit Unterbrechung in strikter Horizontale langsam nach links bewegt. Ein Außerhalb des aktuell Sichtbaren existiert nicht, noch nicht einmal virtuell. Auch die Bewegung von rechts nach links widerspricht den Konventionen filmischer Repräsentation, denn auch Filmbilder werden üblicherweise von links nach rechts gelesen. So stolpert der Blick gleich am Anfang in die falsche Richtung. Überdies ist es allein die Kamera, die sich in diesem kontinuierlichen Ereignisraum bewegt, während die Figuren wie festgefroren dastehen. Resultat ist der Eindruck einer diskontinuierlichen Bewegung, die wirkt wie eine Sukzession von Standbildern, obschon der Film nur aus zwei langen Einstellungen besteht. Im Gegensatz zur Montage, die das Bild wechselt, verändert diese langsame Fahrt es nur und lässt die Szene wie ein farbiges Panorama an der Kamera entlang gleiten.

Doch geht es bei *Chun Tian* nicht allein um die Defiktionalisierung des Illusionismus durch die Durchbrechung der Bedingungen der fließenden Bewegung. Die direkt in das Zelluloid implementierten Untertitel betonen vielmehr die Flächigkeit des filmischen Bildes, wenn sie sich wie eine Membran auf den Bildträger legen und das Dahinterliegende als artifizielle Repräsentation markieren. Der einzige Schnitt ist zudem der klassische *match-cut*, der dialektische Schnitt, der zwei verschiedene Szenen durch Wiederholung oder Duplizierung der Handlung und der Form miteinander verbindet. Indem er zwei Varianten des Gleichen präsentiert, lenkt er den Blick auf die formalen Korrespondenzen wie Differenzen, die dieses Umkehrverhältnis konstituiert. So wird beispielsweise die fundamentale Dichotomie von Stimme und Schrift, Präsenz und Repräsentation, in die Randzone des Films verlagert und damit außer Kraft gesetzt. Die Schrift als materielle Markierung steht für das Außen, für die nachträgliche Zufügung der Übersetzung. Sie figuriert als *Supplement* [02] der abwesenden Stimme, während die Stimme als Indikator körperlicher Anwesenheit gilt. In *Chun Tian* sind jedoch sowohl die Schrift des Untertitels als auch die Stimme externe Zufügungen. Auch die Stimme befindet sich im Außerhalb des Bildes; auch sie ist nachträgliche Zufügung und Supplement der Schrift. Im Off befindet sie sich außerhalb des Bildes und der Zeit. Sie gehört nicht zu der anwesenden Person, sondern ist allein gebunden an den Text. Dazu kommt der Transfer von der einen Sprache zur anderen, der die hierarchische Struktur des Vorher/Nachher revidiert. Der Untertitel übersetzt, was gesagt wird; wenn, wie in der zweiten Variante, erst nach seiner Einblendung gesprochen wird, ist es hingegen die Sprache, die als Übersetzung der Schrift figuriert. So ergänzt das eine das andere, und sowohl Stimme als auch Schrift erscheinen als Zeichen, die eine Absenz aufzufüllen vorgeben. Doch ihre Funktion

02 JAQUES DERRIDA: *GRAMMATOLOGIE*, FRANKFURT/M. 1974. S. 250 F.

ist nicht substitutiv, sondern rein additiv. Dem Bild als Träger von Sinn und Bedeutung bleiben sie jedenfalls merkwürdig fremd.

Weil die Personen auch nur Bausteine innerhalb des symmetrischen Bildfeldes sind, ausgewählte Koordinaten und Richtungsvektoren einer perfekten Komposition, die sich dem Rahmen eingeschrieben hat, kümmert es allerdings niemanden so richtig, wer spricht.

EWIG UND EIN TAG

Gegenüber dieser malerischen Abstraktion entwickelt das nachfolgende Werk fast schon Spielfilmqualitäten. *Forever and Ever* (1995) ist ein Film über Film, so wie *I'm Coming Home in Forty Days* zwei Jahre später ein Film über Malerei sein wird: unbekannte, aber irgendwie auch vertraute Bilder, die keine Zitate sind, aber wie eine ästhetische Verfremdung des Bekannten wirken. Die Referenzen heißen weniger Malerei als Kino. Auch dessen historisch und kulturell codierten Sehweisen ist jedoch nicht so einfach zu entkommen, denn die Frage nach der Geschichte, die ein Film erzählt, ist auch die Frage nach den Regeln, denen er unterliegt. Daher formuliert sich die Dekonstruktion der Bilder und der sie organisierenden Strukturen so nahe wie möglich an diesen selbst, an den Bausteinen der Genres, seinen Manierismen und etablierten Codes. Als abstrakte Auseinandersetzung mit dem Erbe Hollywoods, der Soap Opera und dem indischen Kino der großen Gesten und Gefühle ist *Forever and Ever* andererseits aber auch ein Film der permanenten Verweigerung, der andeutet, ohne Konsequenzen zu ziehen, und Fragmente einer Geschichte erzählt, die gar nicht existiert. Er kennt zwar die Form des Narrativen als Spiel der Differenz, zeigt diese aber allein als leere Kontur.

In der Zergliederung der filmischen Grammatik und Freisetzung ihrer konventionellen Elemente skelettieren de Rijke/de Rooij die von der Filmgeschichte vorgegebene Matrix beinah bis zum Äußersten; übrig bleibt eine Struktur, die als visueller Remix des Bekannten allein im Dazwischen der Einstellungen noch die Idee des Erzählbaren konserviert. Das macht die Rückübersetzung der Bilder in Sprache, die immer ein Problem ist, extra diffizil, denn es gibt kein narratives Raster, auf das die Beschreibung ausweichen könnte. "Handlung" erweist sich vielmehr als Nebenprodukt der additiven Reihung der Bilder; die narrative Ordnung wird zum Produkt der existierenden Lücken, die gerade in ihrer Funktion als Abwesenheit die Oberflächenhandlung konstituieren. Damit präsentiert der Film letztlich Bruchstücke einer cineastischen Ästhetik, die aus der

Abstraktion der Bilder und der filmischen Grammatik ihre Variation des immer Gleichen konstruiert.

Forever and Ever operiert mit den Faktoren Rahmen, Zeit und Raum in einer Weise, die das Sichtbare nicht als Ausschnitt behandelt, sondern als Setzung und Fragment einer virtuellen Totalität. Das Framing der Bilder bewirkt eine Frontalität ohne Hintergrund, die den Film als Film erscheinen lässt: ein zweidimensionales Zeichensystem, das eine pikturale wie referentielle Relation zur Wirklichkeit aufweist, dessen grundlegende Orientierung jedoch die an der physischen Präsenz des Betrachters ist, der das "Außerhalb" des Bildes einzig als imaginäres Museum aus Film und Fernsehen kennt.

Die erste Kamerabewegung umschreibt stets auch eine Topografie des Sehens, wenn sie einen Raum konstruiert, in dem die Szene der Darstellung fest für den Blick auf diese Szene verankert wird. Dieser erste Raum steht hier ganz im Zeichen der Malerei, wenn *Forever and Ever* mit einem langsamen Schwenk über eine indische Bucht mit dem schönen Namen "The Queen´s Necklace" beginnt, bei dem die Horizontlinie genau in der Bildmitte liegt. Himmel und Meer liegen als abstrakt blaue Flächen fast monochrom übereinander; auch als die städtische Skyline ins Bild rückt, bleibt die dominante Farbe blau. Durch die weit geöffnete Blende verliert das Panorama, das der langsame Schwenk zeichnet, alle Tiefe und Horizont. Wenn die nachfolgende Einstellung das Gesicht einer Frau in Nahaufnahme zeigt, könnte der Kontrast deshalb kaum größer sein; diese Frau vor der Bucht, das ist das klassische Porträt mit plastisch modelliertem Vorder- und verschwimmendem Hintergrund. In der Malerei herrscht eine klare Differenzierung der innerbildlichen Schärfe, die sich auf parallele und sukzessive Bildebenen erstreckt, von denen jede autonom ist und von nebeneinander befindlichen Elementen bestimmt. Jede Bildebene, allen voran der Vordergrund, besitzt ihr eigenes Thema und ihren eigenen Wert im Gesamtthema und doch fügen sich alle zu einem Ganzen zusammen. Strukturell bilden

Landschaft und Gesicht deshalb ein Korrelat, in dem die Landschaft in Abhängigkeit vom Gesicht plaziert und das eine wie das andere behandelt wird. Auch die Nahaufnahme im Film erhebt das Gesicht zur Landschaft, moduliert von Licht und Schatten.

Das Gesicht ist das reine Rohmaterial des Affekts, übercodierte, vom Körper getrennte Oberfläche, die sich vom Kopf deterritorialisiert.[03] Doch der Affekt, den das Gesicht der Frau produziert, ist hier nichts anderes als das Wissen betrachtet zu werden, ganz zum Bild geworden zu sein. Sie steht auf dem Balkon eines der Häuser an der Bucht, gerahmt von der Vertikalen des Balkons, der als architektonisches Raster und innerbildliche Rahmung neue ästhetische Grenzziehungen vornimmt. Zunächst blickt sie den Betrachter direkt an, dann aber auch nach rechts aus dem Bild heraus: Frontalansicht, Halbprofil, Profil. Die Bucht scheint transformiert in dunstigen Hintergrund, und auch der Ton, der anfangs deutlich präsent war, reduziert sich auf dezentes Hintergrundrauschen. Räumliche Tiefe entsteht allein noch durch die Überlagerung verschiedener Raumschichten; das Bild selbst präsentiert sich in seiner Komposition als zweidimensionales Tableau.

Dieser Anfang ist eigentlich ein klassischer "Establishing Shot", der den Schauplatz des Geschehens zeigt und die Protagonistin vorstellt allerdings mit einer Insistenz auf der Bildlichkeit, die allem eine mit keiner narrativen Struktur in Verbindung stehende ikonische Qualität verleiht. Dennoch tauchen die gängigen Parameter des konventionellen Kinos alle irgendwann auf: die Landschaft als metaphorischer Fluchtraum des Städters, der Spaziergang entlang eines Sees, der investigative Rundgang durch eine menschenleere Villa, und schließlich das große, romantische Finale in sternklarer Nacht. Und es sind gerade diese kinematografischen Codes und Konventionen, die den

---

03 VGL. GILLES DELEUZE / FÉLIX GUATTARI: "DAS JAHR NULL – GESCHICHTLICHKEIT". IN: VOLKER BOHN (HG.): BILDLICHKEIT. FRANKFURT/M. 1990. S. 438F. SIEHE AUCH DELEUZE: DAS BEWEGUNGS-BILD, A.A.O., S. 143 FF.

Bildern eine semiotische wie ästhetische Aufladung verleihen, die sie letztlich zu einer imaginären Einheit bindet.

Deshalb können fast statische Bilder nichts anderes zeigen als die Dinge selbst, während eine Abfolge von Landschaftspanoramen in *slow motion* von einer Serie menschenleerer Interieurs abgelöst wird, die eher die Idee einer Villa formulieren, als dass sie diese konkret zeigen. Doch die Demontage der dem Film immanenten Illusion erfolgt prompt durch die Division der Kohärenz des filmischen Ganzen in separate Einheiten. Als Film ist *Forever and Ever* in mehr oder weniger gleich lange Sequenzen geordnet, die von Schwarzbildern voneinander getrennt werden und abstrakte Blöcke bilden, Blöcke, die den Lauf eines Tages wiedergeben: die Bucht am Morgen, der See, das Haus, der Himmel bei Nacht.

Indien, wo der Film gedreht wurde, ist hier nah und fern zugleich, genau wie die Landschaftsbilder der frühen Reisenden ihre Impressionen von der Ferne immer mit dem Referenzrahmen des Heimischen versehen. In unserer Globalkultur scheint das kaum mehr nötig, wenn man die Alterität des Anderen nicht dezidiert zum Sujet erheben will. Das Überall merkwürdig exterritorialer Nicht-Orte hat nichts vom anthropologischen Interesse des Europäers für das Exotische. Statt dessen richtet sich ein distanzierter Blick auf abstrakte Landschafts- und Architekturpanoramen, die real und fremd zugleich anmuten. Jetzt scheint irgendwie immer das Gleiche im Anderen auf, andererseits aber auch das Besondere im Allgemeinen. Das bedeutet keinen formalistischen Rückgriff auf einen strukturellen Universalismus, der alle Orte in ein Nirgends verwandelt.

Der Verzicht auf die kulturelle Differenz und Spezifität reproduziert vielmehr die Strukturen der alludierten filmischen Genres selbst, die ihrerseits mit jener kapitalistischen Logik der Globalisierung verschränkt sind.

Deren klassische Determinanten von Handlung und Personen, in dem der Raum ein zu durchquerender und die Zeit eine verfließende ist, werden jedoch konsequent zunichte gemacht von der Struktur distanziert reflektierter Beobachtung. Bei de Rijke/de Rooij laufen die Leute auf die Kamera zu und dann einfach aus dem Bild heraus. Menschen unterhalten sich, ohne dass deutlich wird, worum es eigentlich geht und auch die Personen im Bild selbst bleiben stumm. Irritierend erscheint, dass die bevorzugte Kommunikationsform Stimmen aus dem Off sind, ohne dass eine sichtbare Beziehung zwischen Bild und Stimme besteht. Doch gerade weil sie nicht diegetisch sind, scheinbar nicht zur Handlung gehören, vermögen diese Stimmen die Einstellungen zu verbinden, ohne sie einer narrativen Logik zu unterwerfen. Wenn jemand den sichtbaren Raum zu den Seiten in Richtung jenes visuell negierten Raumes außerhalb des Rahmens verlässt, bleibt er in *Forever and Ever* darin verschwunden. Das Kino insistiert förmlich darauf, dass das Feld des Sichtbaren auch ein Außerhalb, einen virtuellen Raum jenseits des aktuell Sichtbaren besitzt. Erst die Kontinuität der Fiktion als Logik der Narration und plausible Abfolge der Ereignisse definiert im Erzählkino den Ort des Zuschauers als Ort des Geschehens. De Rijke/de Rooij hingegen halten den Zuschauer auf Distanz, wenn sie das Narrative allein im leeren Raum zwischen den Bildern stattfinden lassen. Hier gibt es kein voneinander geschiedenes Hier und Dort, sondern nur die Aktualität des jeweils Sichtbaren.

Außenaufnahmen wirken wie großformatige Fotografien mit cinematischer Präsenz, die in der minimalen Sukzession der Kamerabewegung die Aura lang anschaubarer Tafelbilder tragen und deren flächige Komposition die Natur in die Nähe von Panoramen rückt.
Als Filmbild sind sie rein ikonische Bilder, semiotisierter Landschaftsraum und stereotype "site" zugleich. Doch nicht nur die Landschaft erscheint episch, auch die Menschen in *Forever and Ever* werden wie Dinge gefilmt mit der gleichen ruhig beobachtenden Distanz, die aufzeichnet wie der Blick langsam vertraut wird mit dem, was er sieht. Wie schon in *Chun Tian* geht es auch hier immer wieder um die

Schönheit, die eben nicht nur die der Frau sondern, auch die des Bildes ist. In *Forever and Ever* ist es ein Paar, das am Ufer eines Sees steht, während das Wasser die beiden als ornamentale Struktur umrahmt: "It's beautiful, isn't it?" – "Yes, it's very beautiful." Schön ist nicht nur der See, sondern auch das Bild der Menschen vor dem See. Denn der Kommentar ist ein Kommentar aus dem Off, der zwar ein Dialog der beiden sein könnte, aber auch ein Dialog über die beiden als filmische Komposition.[04] So verschieben sich immer wieder Filmtext und Metatext, Blick in das Bild und Blick auf das Bild als abstraktes Tableau. Doch auch hier naht das Ende, wenn der Betrachter anfängt, sich in Schönheit zu verlieren.

Ein plötzlicher Schnitt, und dann richtet sich die Kamera bereits auf einen neuen Schauplatz des Geschehens, das nie stattfinden wird: das Interieur in seiner verfremdeten Alltäglichkeit.

Die architektonische Inventarisierung beginnt mit einer klassischen Außenaufnahme von der Gartenseite her, dann ist in streng zentral-perspektivischen Einzelaufnahmen ein Raum mit Sofas zu sehen, ein Esszimmer, ein Kaminzimmer, der Blick durch die Glasfront auf den Garten. Fragmente des Raums werden in verschiedenen Einstellungen präsentiert, ohne dass ihre Addition jedoch den Eindruck einer homogenen Situation transportiert. Was sich in langen unbewegten Einstellungen wie ein Nacheinander distinkter Räume präsentiert, setzt der nachfolgende langsame Schwenk vielmehr zu einem einzigen Interieur zusammen: Der Esstisch steht neben dem Terrassenfenster, daneben sind die Sofas, der Kamin zu sehen. Alles wirkt verlassen, unbewohnt, und auch das Klingeln des Telefons, das die ganze Sequenz begleitet, wird nie beantwortet. Alltag scheint in diesem Raum keine Rolle zu spielen. Doch die Kamera, die stets im

---

04 DIE SZENE AM SEE IST IM ÜBRIGEN EIN ZITAT AUS PETER YATES FILM *BULLITT* (USA 1968). HIER GEHT ES GERADE NICHT UM DIE SCHÖNHEIT, SONDERN DIE DESILLUSIONIERUNG ANGESICHTS DER GEWALT, DER DER PROTAGONIST ALS POLIZIST TÄGLICH AUSGESETZT IST. INSOFERN IST ES DER KONTRAST ZWISCHEN DEM BILD UND DEM TEXT, DER DAS BILD STRUKTURIERT.

Modus des Konstativums operiert, forscht weiter und entdeckt eine Treppe, die eine Etage höher führt. Ein Schwenk durch das Schlafzimmer fixiert in der Tat Spuren von Anwesenheit: ein offensichtlich benutztes Bett, herumliegende Kleidungsstücke. Und vor allem – das Telefon hört auf zu klingeln. Was noch fehlt bei dem in statische Fragmente zerlegten Rundgang durch die Villa ist der Swimming Pool auf der Dachterrasse. Auch hier finden sich vermeintliche Indizien von Präsenz. Doch dann fängt das Telefon wieder an zu läuten und alles ist genauso unbestimmt wie vorher. So läuft die Spannung immer wieder ins Leere zugunsten von Bildern, die alles versprechen aber nie einlösen, weil sie eben nur Bilder ohne eindeutige Evidenz sind.

Was der zweite Blick jedoch offenbart, ist die Re/vision des einen Bildes durch das andere, der einen Sequenz durch die nachfolgende, und die Offensichtlichkeit des Genres selbst, die dazu auffordert, seine Regularien zu befragen. Die Bilder erzeugen die Illusion linearer Kohärenz, wenn man sie mit dem narrativen Film assoziiert und beginnt, die Einstellungen als Folge zusammenhängender Ereignisse zu lesen. Doch das Ganze ist auch hier mehr als die Summe seiner Teile, wenn das in Einzeltableaus fragmentierte Interieur eine architektonische Dimension suggeriert, die sich als Produkt serieller Addition zwangsläufig auflöst im totalisierenden Schwenk. Als realistischer Schauplatz ist dieser Raum zwar durch seine Teile definiert deren Anschlüsse gemäß filmischer Konvention von vornherein festgelegt sind, diese können sich aber in alle Richtungen zusammenfügen. Letztlich bleibt er eine gestaltlose Entität die alles, was sich in ihr ereignet hat oder ereignen könnte, eliminiert hat zugunsten des reinen Potentials der Leere.[05]

Die letzte Sequenz von *Forever and Ever* ist deshalb als absoluter Gegensatz zu dieser räumlichen wie affektiven Unbestimmtheit konstruiert – Außen – statt Innenraum, Natur statt Kultur, Menschen statt Leere, Stimmen statt Geräusch. Im Referenzsystem der Kunst bedeutet dies eine Rückkehr zur Metaphysik der Romantik, zum *chiaroscuro* der Landschaftsmalerei, zum dramatisch inszenierten Hell-Dunkel. Der Intensitätsgrad der Farbe und des Lichts absorbiert jede fest konturierte Form und die Landschaft verwandelt sich in die unendliche Weite des Raums. Allein das Licht eines Lagerfeuers leuchtet am Ende die Gesichter der Darsteller aus und präzisiert aus dem dunklen Hintergrund der Nacht im extremen Gegenlichteffekt die Konturen zweier Jungen, die die Sterne beobachten. In *Forever and Ever* ist dieses Spiel mit dem Licht des Lagerfeuers erhebend-schön und voll metaphysischem Kitsch, ein präzise geplanter Romantizismus aus dem Herzen der Illusionsmaschine Kino. Licht, Dunkelheit und die unendliche Weite des Firmaments mit seinen Sternen: "Every star may be a sun to someone."

Nachdem die Dinge im Kino ihre Sichtbarkeit gegen ihre Bedeutung und ihre Präsenz gegen die Dynamik der Geschichte eingetauscht haben, verwandeln de Rijke/de Rooij die Bilder letztlich wieder in den Rohstoff der Imagination zurück. Die konkrete Zeichenebene verschiebt sich ins Imaginäre und wieder zurück. Die Unterscheidungslinie des Films von der Wirklichkeit liegt deshalb in der optionalen Besetzung des Blicks, der immer auch ein anderer sein könnte. Ähnliches gilt für die Geräusche, die nicht mehr funktional sind, sondern sich verselbständigt haben zur eigenen Funktion. Das Telefon, das man nie zu sehen bekommt, hat allein den Zweck, durch seine Abwesenheit auf die Kategorie von Abwesenheit zu verweisen, wenn es als akustisches Signal durch den Leerraum seiner fehlenden

05 DARIN LIEGT DIE EIGENTLICHE AFFINITÄT NICHT NUR ZU DEN STEREOTYPEN RAUMKULISSEN DER SOAP OPERA, SONDERN DER SPEZIFISCHEN BESETZUNG VON RÄUMEN IN DEN FILMEN VON MICHELANGELO ANTONIONI, DER SEINE GRÖSSTEN RESONANZEFFEKTE AUS DER GEGENÜBERSTELLUNG VON BEVÖLKERTEM UND LEEREM RAUM GEWINNT. ANTONIONI ERHEBT, VOR ALLEM AUCH DURCH DEN EINSATZ DER ALLES ABSORBIERENDEN FARBE, DEN RAUM ZU EINER POTENZ DER LEERE, NACHDEM DAS GESCHEHEN SICH REALISIERT UND ZUM ABSCHLUSS GEKOMMEN IST. DIE AFFEKTIVE INSTANZ IST ALLEIN DIE DES VON SEINEN KOORDINATEN BEFREITEN RAUMS, DER BIS ZUR VOLLSTÄNDIGEN LEERE UND ZUM BEINAH NICHT-FIGURATIVEN *ABSTRACT* GETRIEBEN WIRD. VGL. AUCH DELEUZE: *DAS BEWEGUNGS-BILD,* A.A.O., S. 165FF.

bildlichen Präsenz hallt. Diese Leere ist jedoch nicht allein Leere als Absenz, sondern eine kulissenhafte Leere, die als Mangel an festgeschriebener Bedeutung scheinbar nur darauf wartet, dass die Fiktion von ihr Besitz ergreift. Die Abwesenheit des Fehlenden ist praktisch als Eigenschaft des Gegenwärtigen zu sehen. In dieser imaginären Präsenz des Fiktiven artikuliert sich die eigentliche Differenz als *différance*, als verschiebende Aufschiebung von Sinn und Bedeutung und unentscheidbare Alternation der Perspektive der Struktur und der des Ereignisses. Kontexte werden zwar nicht völlig eliminiert, aber heruntergefahren auf ein Minimum. Die Bucht, das ist ein Versprechen, die Landschaft das Setting für einen Krimi, das Haus bietet die diffuse Suspense und die Lagerfeuer-Romantik eine Intimität hart am Klischee in Technicolor. Das Genre setzt die Standards, der Rest sind Bilder und deren Polysemie; Sinn entsteht allein durch die sich übereinanderlegenden Schichten aus Zufall und Bedeutung. Letztlich ist diese Fixierung auf raum- und zeitgreifende Ordnungsmuster aber auch eine Form der Realitätsaneignung, die einem Verlust an Realität gleichkommt. Deshalb auch das unbestimmte Gefühl der Melancholie, des Verlusts (von Sinn?) in der Abstraktion von allem Eindeutigen in der Welt der instabilen Zeichen.

Nach dieser Auseinandersetzung mit der Syntagmatik des Filmischen in seiner konventionalisierten Form, in der Inhalt und Emotion sich aus standardisierter Topik und standardisierten Codes konstituieren, verschieben sich mit *Voor Bas Oudt* die Parameter ein wenig mehr in Richtung Sinnlichkeit und Semantik. *Voor Bas Oudt* [06] (1996) verlässt den diskursiven Raum der Möglichkeiten und Multiplikationen mit seinem virtuellen Horizont ständig zurückweichender Bedeutung. Damit ist eine Wendung, wenn auch keine Kurskorrektur markiert, die bislang erprobten Parameter noch weiter zu reduzieren und die

06 DER TITEL IST EINE WIDMUNG AN EINEN LEHRER VON DE RIJKE / DE ROOIJ AUS DER RIETVELD-ACADEMIE AMSTERDAM.

Spuren des Narrativen aufgehen zu lassen in der reinen Präsenz des Bildes. Dass der Film allein aus einer Plansequenz besteht und ohne Montage auskommt, resultiert auch aus seiner Kürze von einer Minute. Doch auch der Zugriff auf die Wirklichkeit ist hier weniger dekonstruierend als phänomenologisch, wenn die Kamera ganz in den Dienst des Registrierens externer Strukturen und Oberflächen tritt.

Am Anfang von *Voor Bas Oudt* steht eine abstrakt geometrische Struktur fächerförmig angeordneter Linien, die konzentrisch nach außen verlaufen als ornamentale Konfiguration an der Grenze zum Nicht-Figurativen. Die intensive grüne Farbe absorbiert geradezu den Gegenstand. Im Umkreis der Struktur wird jedoch erkennbar, dass es sich um das Blattwerk einer tropischen Pflanze handelt. Die Kamera tastet sich an deren Oberfläche entlang und fokussiert ein Blatt, auf dem ein weißer Schmetterling sitzt, ein Nachtfalter. Dieser flattert leicht mit den Flügeln, hält für einen Moment zitternd inne und schließt dann langsam seine Flügel.

Aufgenommen wurde der Film mit einem Boroskop, wie es auch für wissenschaftliche Aufnahmen verwendet wird, da es über extreme Tiefenschärfe verfügt. Mit dieser Kamera können selbst in der extremen Vergrößerung alle Raumebenen ohne Verzerrung reproduziert werden. Durch die regelmäßige Schärfe der Oberflächen entwickeln sich alle Elemente zu einem gleichermaßen anschaubaren Ereignis. Zunächst sind es die innerbildlichen Strukturen, die ins Auge fallen: das Muster auf den Schmetterlingsflügeln mit seinem Netzwerk schwarzer Linien, die Struktur und Materialität des plastischen Blattwerks und die zarte Fragilität des Insekts. *Voor Bas Oudt* scheint eine Momentaufnahme zu sein, eine kurze Studie zur Sichtbarmachung visueller Qualitäten, und doch erfüllt er kein Kriterium wissenschaftlicher Dokumentation. Gerade in der Konzentration auf das eine Bild des Schmetterlings erfährt dieser vielmehr eine konnotative Aufladung, die nur im Film möglich ist. In der langsamen Beobachtung entwickelt sich eine ganze poetische Semiologie der Stoffe und

Körper, der Ornamente, Farben und Texturen.

Wie schon in *Chun Tian* endet jedoch auch dieser kurze Film unerwartet und scheinbar zu früh; eben noch war der Blick auf den Schmetterling gerichtet, dann hebt das Schwarz des Filmstreifens jede referentielle Illusion von Wirklichkeit auf und transformiert das Bild allein in ein Erinnerungsbild. Auch *Voor Bas Oudt* kennt nur den unvollendeten Augenblick als Erfüllungspunkt in der Zeit, als leeren Zeitpunkt innerhalb einer linearen Struktur. Der existenzielle, metaphysische Augenblick als Finalität der Handlung ist ihm fremd; hier gibt es nur den abrupten Bruch in der filmischen Zeit, die allein im Imaginären ihre Fortsetzung finden kann. Als kalkulierter Schnitt mit der Realität der Illusion – aufhören, wenn es am Schönsten ist – stellt er aber auch einen Bezug zum Symbolsystem der Ikonografie her, auf das das Bild des Schmetterlings letztlich rekurriert.

Wie in der Mimesis der Malerei sind die Dinge, was sie sind, aber eben auch noch etwas mehr. Schmetterlinge bevölkern die Stilleben des niederländischen Barock, denn sie sind das perfekte Sinnbild der Vanitas, der Vergänglichkeit alles Irdischen. Der Schmetterling erinnert an die Unmöglichkeit der Ewigkeit und die ewige Entropie. Er zelebriert den Augenblick, der ein transitorischer ist – doch in dieser Vergänglichkeit spiegelt sich auch die vergehende Zeit, die der Film in seiner Kürze dokumentiert. Ein Moment der Schönheit nach der Metamorphose (der Nachtfalter ist eben aus seinem Kokon geschlüpft), dann ist dieser Moment auch schon vorbei. Metaphorisch symbolisiert der Schmetterling die drei ontologischen Manifestationen der Zeit von Sein, Werden und Präsenz in ihrer Materialisation als Form, Erscheinen und Existenz.[07] Der Prozess des Vergehens – denn nichts anderes spricht so gelehrt aus der Ikonografie der Vanitas – ist deshalb auch eine Variante der Topik der Zeit, die sich in ihrer tragischen Endlichkeit präsentiert. Doch wie die Vanitas ihre Botschaft der Metaphysik des Todes in Bildern diskreter

07 VGL. MICHEL ONFRAY: *DIE FORMEN DER ZEIT. THEORIE DES SAUTERNES*. BERLIN 1999. S. 120.

Schönheit sublimiert, ist auch dieser Schmetterling in seinem tropischen Mikrokosmos vor allem präsent in der affirmierenden Schönheit der Zeit des Jetzt.

REALISTISCHE ABSTRAKTION

Wörter benennen Dinge, andererseits konstituieren sich aber auch die Dinge durch die Sprache; ohne Signifikant kein Signifikat. Sprache ist nicht als Abbildung eines vorgängig vorhandenen Objekts zu verstehen, das in der Sprache seine Bezeichnung findet. Erst dadurch, dass etwas benannt – kommuniziert – wird, erhält dieses Etwas vielmehr seine diskursivierte Form, die es als Zeichen verhandelbar macht. Ähnliches gilt für den Raum, dessen Realität sich in der Wahrnehmung seiner Grenzen konstituiert. In Referenz zu anderen Dingen, primär denen der eigenen Erfahrung, formiert er sich und erlangt Gestalt.

Eines der Lieblingsbeispiele der Linguistik für die Strukturierung der Sprache durch Erfahrung, die Einschreibung der spezifisch kulturellen Wahrnehmung in die Kommunikation, lautet denn auch: Die Sprache der Eskimos kennt fast zwanzig verschiedene Wörter für Schnee. Da dieser für die Bewohner der nördlichen Polarregion eine zentrale Kategorie bildet, benennen sie ihn exakt in seinen verschiedenen Diversifikationen. Die *inuit* besitzen eine sprachliche Phänomenologie des Schnees, die dem europäischen Verständnis völlig fremd ist, denn unsere Sprache reduziert auf ein summarisches Konzept, was als Vorstellungsbild nur schwach ausgebildet ist. Das Reale und seine Bilder provozieren also Begriffe und Begriffe Bilder. Jenseits der Dichotomie von Realität und Subjektivität, Anschein und Bedeutung, Signifikat und Signifikant ist jedoch der Film, oder besser noch: das kinematografische Bild, scheinbar in der Lage, eine eigene Ordnung im Sichtbaren zu produzieren, in der das Bild sich gegen den Begriff behaupten kann.[08] Denn nur im Bild ist die Lesbarkeit des Zeichens unmittelbar an seine reine Sichtbarkeit gebunden. Was im Film auf Ebene des Sichtbaren stattfindet, ist Resultat eines strukturierten Zugriffs auf das Reale, insofern der Film den Dingen eine Visualität verleiht, die nicht nur auf der substantiellen Abwesenheit dieser Dinge und der daraus resultierenden

08 VGL. KÖTZ: *DER TRAUM, DIE SEHNSUCHT UND DAS KINO*, A.A.O., S. 83.

repräsentativen Differenz gründet, sondern als Double des Realen auch eine ständige Verschiebung konstituiert. Darin liegt der fundamentale Unterschied in der Konstruktion "realer" und filmischer Realität, Welt-Bildern und Bild-Welten, hinsichtlich ihrer Effekte und Rekonfiguration des Wirklichen.

I'm Coming Home In Forty Days (1997), der während einer vierwöchigen Reise zur Disko Bay in Grönland entstand, ist ein Film über die Zeit und die Wahrnehmung der Zeit, so wie der Eisberg, um den es geht, ein Stück eingefrorene Vergangenheit ist.
Das schimmernde Eis in seiner bloßen Existenz repräsentiert die konstante Transition des aktuellen Begriffs von Zeit. Die Kategorie Zeit hat hier jedoch auch unmittelbar mit der kognitiven Aneignung der Dinge zu tun, der Art, wie wir sie begreifen und mnemotechnisch fixieren, denn Zeit und Erinnerung laufen in parallelen Bahnen. Die mediale Aufzeichnung versucht die Unwiederbringlichkeit des Gesehenen zu unterlaufen, das in seiner prozessualen Qualität später lediglich erinnert werden kann. Insofern geht es in *I'm Coming Home in Forty Days* auch um die Auslotung der Grenze der Re/präsentation als Wiedervergegenwärtigung von etwas Vergangenem und die strukturelle Ähnlichkeit von Bild und Erinnerung als von Projektionen durchzogene und niemals ganz realistische Ab- und Einbildung. Dokumentarisch formuliert ein Film das Vorgegebene zur Prägnanz, indem er das, was man schon ahnte, im Medium des bewegten Bildes zur Gewissheit erhebt. Er operiert innerhalb von vordefinierten Einstellungen, filmischen Codes und Semiotisierungen und gewinnt seine Evidenz aus diesen. *I'm Coming Home In Forty Days* hingegen stellt sich eine wesentlich abstraktere Frage: Dieselbe Prägnanz zu erzeugen mit etwas, das unvorgewusst ist, das heißt, das bisher nicht Erkannte zur Erkennung zu bringen, ohne das Sehen auf den Akt des Wiedererkennens zu reduzieren.
Der Eisberg wird erst in der Abbildung und dann nochmals in der Wahrnehmung dieser Abbildung rekonstruiert. Deshalb ist es in

diesem Fall auch möglich, im Nachhinein die Realität über das Abbild zu rekonstruieren, wobei immer eine Differenz zwischen Realem und Repräsentation bestehen bleibt, eine Differenz, die nicht nur Resultat der medialen Verfremdung ist, sondern auch der stetig sich verändernden Erfahrungsgewissheit. Formal besteht dieser Film aus nichts anderem als drei unterschiedlich langen Einstellungen eines Eisbergs, der langsam von einem Schiff umrundet wird. Damit trägt er die gleiche Struktur wie ein Triptychon, das sich über visuelle wie zeitliche Bezüge und Verschiebungen in der Sukzession entfaltet. Während das klassische Triptychon jedoch das Konstrukt einer zeitlichen Folge des Vorher und Nachher jeweils in den Seitenflügeln und des Jetzt in der zentralen Mitteltafel zeigt, also eine Zuwendung des Augenblicks zu seinem chronologischen Rahmen der Vergangenheit und der Zukunft präsentiert, überträgt der Film, dem das zeitliche Moment implizit ist, dieses Konzept auf die räumliche Dimension. In *I'm Coming Home In Forty Days* ist es die Interferenz verschiedener Perspektiven, die unterschiedliche Wahrnehmungsfelder desselben repräsentieren. Das meint weniger ein Spiel mit der Referenz als Durchspielen von Seh- und Bildmöglichkeiten als den Versuch einer Erschließung des Gegenstandes in der ästhetischen Erfahrung. Die visuelle Totalität ergibt sich erst aus jenem Zusammenspiel der Singularitäten, die das Jetzt der Wahrnehmung in Hinblick auf die Vergangenheit und Zukunft als Ausdruck eines raumzeitlichen Kontinuums inszenieren.

Die Aufnahmen zu dem Film entstanden am frühen Morgen bei diesigem Himmel; immer wieder lösen sich die stereometrischen Grundformen des Eisbergs auf, verändern ihr Erscheinungsbild in der wechselnden Lichtperspektive und verschmelzen mit dem Grau-Weiß des Himmels. In dem schwer zu verortenden Raum aus diffusem Licht gerinnt alle feste Substanz zu einem transitorischen Übergang von Materie und Atmosphäre. Allein der Gegensatz von Wasser und Eisberg bleibt klar konturiert. Gefilmt wurde zudem im Herbst, wenn das Wasser sich kompakt zu verdichten beginnt.

Die von der Schiffsbewegung produzierten Wellen sind deshalb
eher träge; die ganze Atmosphäre deutet auf Komprimierung,
auf Annäherung der einzelnen Elemente. Da der Standort als Ort
der Kamera sich mit dem Schaukeln des Schiffs kontinuierlich
verschiebt, stellt sich beim Schweifen des Auges über die Landschaft ein leichtes Schwindelgefühl ein. Es ist, als leide man unter
Gleichgewichtsstörungen wenn das betrachtete Objekt keine
genaue Verortung zulässt, und der Blick im Nirgendwo zwischen
Himmel, Eis und schwankendem Horizont verloren geht.
Gefilmt wurde mit einer fest justierten Kamera ohne Schwenk,
die Brennweite des Objektivs auf den Eisberg fokussiert, zu den
Bedingungen der technischen Apparatur, während das Schiff die
Bewegung in der Horizontalen und Vertikalen bestimmt. Das Sehen
gerinnt beim Betrachten dieser Bilder immer wieder zum reinen
Substrat, und das, was es wahrnimmt, scheint einer anderen
Ordnung des Sichtbaren anzugehören.

Nun differiert filmische Sichtbarkeit per se von der Sichtbarkeit im
Realen, da ihr Wesen gerade darin besteht, im diskursiven Raum
der Zeichen die Anwesenheit von etwas Abwesenden zu erzeugen,
indem die Sichtbarkeit des Gegenstandes von seiner substantiellen
Anwesenheit getrennt und einer isolierten (Re-)Präsentation unter-
worfen wird. Film findet dort statt, wo das Reale nicht ist. Als reine
Sichtbarkeit entsubstanzialisiert die Phänomenologie des filmischen
Bildes allerdings die vorgängige Sichtbarkeit, denn sie ist zwar referentiell an diese gebunden, verweist jedoch nicht direkt auf die
Anwesenheit einer Entität. Das liegt daran, dass die direkte Sichtbarkeit des Gegenstandes an eine Welt der Erscheinung gebunden ist,
in der Visualität immer nur die externe Sichtbarkeit der Oberfläche ist.
Außerhalb des Bildes wird die Anschauung durch andere Sinne
ergänzt; im Bild sind Gegenstand und Sichtbarkeit hingegen
identisch, da der Gegenstand des Bildes allein Oberfläche ist.
Insofern konstituiert das Bild eine eigene Wirklichkeit durch die

Verabsolutierung des Sichtbaren zu einem Material ohne Substanz.[09]
In *I'm Coming Home in Forty Days* spielen solche grundsätzlichen
Phänomenologien eine nicht unerhebliche Rolle.
Konzeptuell nutzt der Film die unaufhebbare Differenz zwischen
Sehen und Wissen als Widerspruch zwischen dem, was wir von
dem vorgestellten Gegenstand wissen und dem, was tatsächlich zu
sehen ist. In der Tat entspricht das filmische Bild des Eisbergs nicht
der Vorstellung, die das abstrakte Konzept "Eisberg" evoziert: Weder
zeigt er eine schroffe, zerklüftete Oberfläche, noch präsentiert er sich
als steil aus dem Wasser ragende Erscheinung. Im Gegenteil, der
Eisberg zeichnet sich durch seine sanft gerundeten Formen aus und
wirkt wie eine kompakte Düne in einer Wüste aus Eis, deren Textur
eher an Softeis erinnert als an fest gefrorene Materie. In der langsamen Fahrt um den Berg herum wird deutlich, dass dieser zwei
divergierende Ansichten besitzt, eine glatte Vorderseite und eine
aufgesplitterte Rückseite, eine konkave und eine konvexe
Wölbung. Es fällt schwer, seine tatsächliche Größe zu schätzen;
der Sinn für Maßstab und Dimensionalität geht verloren, denn auch
die reale Umgebung scheint abstrakt und undifferenzierbar. Es gibt
deshalb auch kein Erkennen im Sinne jenes konventionellen Wieder-
erkennungseffekts, bei dem allein kulturelles Wissen re-produziert wird.

Dem Projekt der Grönlandreise und des aus ihr resultierenden
Triptychons über den Eisberg vorgelagert war eine Fotografie von Eis-
bergen in der Polarregion mit ihrer distanziert kühlen Ausstrahlung.
Als Fotografie evozieren diese Eisberge eine eigene, fremdartige
Atmosphäre und erscheinen als plastische Manifestation eingefrorener
Vergangenheit. Sie strahlen eine unmittelbare Präsenz aus, gleich-
wohl wirken sie seltsam irreal, da Eisberge nicht gerade zu den
alltäglichen Anschauungsobjekten unserer Hemisphäre zählen.

09 VGL. LAMBERT WIESING: *DIE SICHTBARKEIT DES BILDES. GESCHICHTE UND PERSPEKTIVEN FORMALER*
ÄSTHETIK. REINBEK BEI HAMBURG 1997. S. 160F.

Als Bild strahlen sie dennoch eine Vertrautheit aus, die sie phänomenologisch gar nicht besitzen. Jeroen de Rijke und Willem de Rooij
interessierte jedoch gerade dieser Moment, in dem das Bild und
das Reale nicht mehr allein referentiell aufeinander bezogen sind,
sondern durch die unmittelbare Erfahrung in ein neues Verhältnis
zueinander gesetzt scheinen. Das durch die Fotografie indirekt Vorge-
wusste legt sich quasi als unsichtbare Membran über die Erfahrung
des Gegenstandes in der aktuellen Wahrnehmung und erzeugt eine
unaufhebbare Distanz zu diesem Wahrgenommenen, die aus dem
Abgleich des aus der Reproduktion Bekannten mit seinem aktuellen
Referenten resultiert. Die visuelle Tatsächlichkeit der grönländischen
Eisberge scheint zunächst denn auch wie eine Wiederholung ihres
fotografischen Abbildes, da keine optische Referenz
zur Verfügung steht, kein Vergleichsmoment der visuellen Erfahrung.
Das Erfassen externer Realität vollzieht sich schließlich primär über
die optische Erfassung der sichtbaren Erscheinungen und ihre sukzessive Abspeicherung als Erinnerungsbilder.

I'm Coming Home In Forty Days befasst sich insofern eher mit der
Syntaktik des Gegenstands als mit seiner Semantik, eher mit dem
Modus des Wahrnehmens und Darstellens als mit dem, was sich als
faktische Gegebenheit zeigt. Das aus verschiedenen Ansichten
sich konstituierende Vorstellungsbild präsentiert sich als Konzept,
das sich mit dem Erfahrungshorizont des Betrachters auflädt und
abstrakte Impressionen mit subjektiver Anschauung verbindet.
Obschon der Film eine äußerst reduzierte Vorstellung des Eisbergs
liefert, zeigt er diese Vorstellung als von der Ästhetik der Malerei
durchdrungene, vergegenwärtigte Erinnerung, die dennoch nur
denjenigen in die Vergangenheit zurückzuführen vermag, der das
Bild tatsächlich gesehen hat.[10]
Dieses Moment der Zeit als Spur der Erinnerung und Gedächtnis-

---

10 VGL. DELEUZE: *DAS ZEIT-BILD*, A.A.O., S. 77.

raum ist konstitutiv für *I'm Coming Home in Forty Days*, der von einer intensiven zeitlichen Langsamkeit getragen wird, durch die sich Bewegung aus dem Bild selbst heraus entwickelt - nicht aus der Montage der Einstellungen. In ihrem dem a-perspektivischen *All-Over* der Malerei sich nähernden Bildraum tragen die langsam sich verändernden Einstellungen dennoch auch die Spur der referentiellen Einschreibung des Tatsächlichen, die Roland Barthes als das Noema der Fotografie beschrieben hat, jenes auf die Faktizität des Dargestellten insistierendes "es ist so gewesen", in dem sich Realität und Vergangenheit verbinden.[11] Diese Insistenz auf eine materielle Wirklichkeit und die Funktion der Fotografie als Index von etwas Dagewesenem meint nicht bloß das dokumentarische Moment der Repräsentation, sondern auch die aus dem Lauf der Zeit abgesonderte Präsenz, die sich jenseits der bloßen Kategorien von Hier und Jetzt dem Bild unwiderruflich eingeschrieben hat. Im Film tritt zu diesem Phänomen jedoch noch zusätzlich eine neue Textur nicht der Form, sondern der Dichte: die Zeit, die Verdichtung in der Temporalisation. In der sukzessiven Erfassung des Eisbergs artikuliert sich die Zeit als jenes reine Zeit-Bild, das Gilles Deleuze benannt hat als pure Darstellung der Zeit, in der diese nicht mehr bloßes Derivat der Bewegung ist, sondern die Bewegung zur Perspektive der Zeit wird.[12] Dieses Zeit-Bild verleiht dem, was sich verändert, eine Form, in der sich die Veränderung ereignet.

11 "DAS, WAS ICH SEHE, BEFAND SICH DORT, AN DEM ORT, DER ZWISCHEN DER UNENDLICHKEIT UND DEM WAHRNEHMENDEN SUBJEKT... LIEGT; ES IST DAGEWESEN UND GLEICHWOHL AUF DER STELLE ABGESONDERT WORDEN; ES WAR GANZ UND GAR, UNWIDERLEGBAR GEGENWÄRTIG." ROLAND BARTHES: *DIE HELLE KAMMER. BEMERKUNGEN ZUR FOTOGRAFIE.* FRANKFURT/M. 1985. S. 87. EINSCHRÄNKEND BLEIBT ALLERDINGS HINZUZUFÜGEN, DASS AUCH BARTHES GERADE IN DER BEWEGUNG DES FILMISCHEN BILDES EINE ENTSCHEIDENDE PHÄNOMENOLOGISCHE DIFFERENZ ERKENNT, DIE SICH VOR ALLEM AUF DAS MOMENT DER POSE ALS STILLGESTELLTE WIRKLICHKEIT AUCH IM MOMENT DER AUFNAHME SELBST BEZIEHT. VGL. EBD., S. 88.

12 VGL. DELEUZE: *DAS ZEIT-BILD*, A.A.O., S. 37.

Das bedeutet auch, dass in dem Augenblick, in dem das kinematografische Bild dem Foto am nächsten kommt, es sich zugleich am
radikalsten von ihm unterscheidet, denn es repräsentiert nicht nur
Zeit als immerwährende Gegenwart, es ist Zeit.[13] Das Tatsächliche
ist nicht stillgestellt in seiner momenthaften, auf die Zukunft
ausstrahlenden Gegenwärtigkeit, sondern festgehalten in seiner transitorischen Präsenz. Das fotografische Bild entsteht aus dem Verlust
des Augenblicks heraus, denn es ist die der Dauer entzogene, reine
Gegenwart. Das filmische Bild hingegen hält die Zeit nicht an, sondern
hebt sie auf in der Präsentation einer ständig Vergangenheit werdenden
Gegenwart. Obschon im Film sich immer alles in der Augenblicklichkeit des Jetzt zu ereignen scheint, sind es an sich immer nur
Sequenzen des Erinnerns, die man sieht. Der Zeit der gegenwärtigen
Erfahrung ist im Film immer schon die Dauer der Vergangenheit eingeschrieben als Gegenwart, die eben gerade nicht gegenwärtig,
sondern bereits abgeschlossen ist. Die Zeitform des Films ist eine
Vergangenheit, die sich als illusionäre Gegenwart inszeniert.

Der Erinnerung als reine Vorstellung steht immer die repräsentative
Funktion des Films im Weg, der keinen Verweis auf außerhalb des
Zeichens Stehendes kennt. Dafür produziert er Bilder, die im langsamen Dahinschwinden jeder Mimesis manchmal eine ganz eigene
Wirklichkeit zur Anschauung bringen. In *I'm Coming Home in Forty
Days* präsentiert sich diese Wirklichkeit wie ein in *slow motion* sich
veränderndes Gemälde, das der Blick nicht auf einmal erfassen
kann. In seiner Abkehr von der geometrisierten Perspektivzentrierung
verlangt es selbst Zeit, um gesehen zu werden. Erst in der Sukzession
der verschiedenen Ansichten fügen sich diese jenes Raster, das
eine rekonstruierende Erschließung des Gesehen als visuelle Totalität
möglich macht, die in ihrer Komplexität dennoch nie vollständig in
anschauliche Begrifflichkeit transformiert werden kann. Durch die

13 VGL. EBD., S. 31.

chromatische Ausdifferenzierung verschiedener Graustufen erhält
das Bild eine opake Dichte, die jede Anstrengung einer Ausdifferenzierung von Tiefenschärfe zunichte macht. Gerade die Abschaffung
der illusionistischen Dreidimensionalität im Dunst der Erscheinung
öffnet diese andererseits jedoch auf die Zeit als vierte Dimension,
in der die dauerhafte Präsenz des Bildes wichtiger wird als seine
Repräsentanz.

Der Titel mit seinem Versprechen: "I'm Coming Home" benennt
die Figur des Reisens, die eine zeitliche ist, und die Entfernung von
einem Ort, zu dem es eine Rückkehr geben wird. Das temporale
Moment verbindet sich auf diese Weise mit dem Topos der Seereise
und deren unspezifischer Ver-Ortung im Raum, der ein zu durchquerender ist. Das Schiff als "schaukelndes Stück Raum", als "Ort ohne
Ort" [14] markiert einen Zustand jenseits territorialer Fixierung, eine
Reise ohne definiertes Ziel, in der die Vorstellung von Bewegung als
Fortbewegung nach konkreten Richtungsvektoren zum Stillstand
kommt. Insofern impliziert der Film in seiner linearen Struktur auch
eine abstrakte Vorstellung von Narrativität. Das Schiff, von dem aus
gefilmt wird, ist immer präsent, als vom Wellengang diktierte, konti-
nuierliche Auf- und Abbewegung in der Horizontalen. Dadurch erhält
das nur minimal sich verändernde Bild eine rhythmische Orchestrie-
rung, die auch den Betrachterstandort als strukturierendes Bewe-
gungsmoment in die Repräsentation integriert.
Frontal ins Bild gerückt, irritiert jedoch bereits die erste Einstellung
eines langsamen Zooms aus dem Bild heraus die üblichen Koordinaten der Raumerfahrung, da der Fluchtpunkt sich in der vertikalen
Schwankung des Bildes nicht eindeutig bestimmen und den
Bild-Raum zur Oberfläche werden lässt. Diese zweidimensionale

14 MICHEL FOUCAULT: "ANDERE ORTE". IN: *AISTHESIS. WAHRNEHMUNG HEUTE ODER PERSPEKTIVEN
EINER ANDEREN ÄSTHETIK.* HG. VON KARLHEINZ BARCK, PETER GENTE, HEIDI PARIS U. STEFAN RICHTER.
LEIPZIG 1990. S. 46.

Oberflächlichkeit stellt den Zoom andererseits jedoch dezidiert in jene Tradition modernistischer Malerei, die die klassische Figur-Grund-Relation mit ihrer hierarchischen Bildordnung in radikale Flächigkeit aufgelöst hat: die monochrome Malerei und mehr noch das *All-Over* des abstrakt expressionistischen Farbraums. Eisberg und Himmel sind in ihrer wahrnehmbaren Erscheinung abstrakte Einheiten, bis ein Teil der Schiffsreling als ästhetische Grenze ins Bild rückt, die den Ort der Kamera als definierte Verortung des Betrachters wieder sichtbar und das Abbildhafte der bildlichen Konfiguration präsent werden lässt. Die zentrale zweite und längste Einstellung ergänzt diese Frontalansicht des Eisbergs um die Daten seiner stereometrischen Dimension, die aufgezeichnet werden auf einer langsamen Fahrt um ihn herum. Diese Fahrt steht ganz im Zeichen einer Ästhetik des Verschwindens, wenn die Grenzziehung zwischen Eisberg und Himmel durchlässig wird und die Ansicht temporär einem visuellen *abstract* weicht. Die bleigraue Farbe treibt den Raum zur Leere, eliminiert seine Koordinaten und absorbiert die Form bis zur Grenze des Nicht-Figurativen. Alle räumliche Fixierung wird beseitigt zugunsten eines nichttotalisierbaren Raums. Allein das Wasser erscheint als glatte, reflektierende Fläche, während die Konturen des Eises sich auflösen, bis sie völlig in den undefinierten Bereich des Himmels übergehen. Diese Diffusion tritt umso deutlicher hervor, als die Grenze zwischen Wasser und Eisberg als dunkle Gerade das Filmbild geometrisch strukturiert – fast schon ein horizontaler "Zip" mit immer wieder aus dem Fokus geratendem Realitätsbezug. In diesem Rekurs auf das Vokabular Barnett Newmans manifestiert sich die eigentliche ästhetische Referenzsemantik von *I'm Coming Home in Forty Days.*

Klassische Gemälde wie Caspar David Friedrichs *Das Eismeer (Die Gescheiterte Hoffnung)* sind zwar, vom Sujet ausgehend, eben-falls ein naheliegender Vergleich, der jedoch gerade in der Differenz zu *I'm Coming Home in Forty Days* dessen abstrakt strukturalen

Realismus verdeutlicht. Friedrichs Eisblöcke sind vor allem Allegorie, destruierte Oberfläche und Sinnbild einer Landschaft in Aufruhr. Sein Gemälde liefert keine exakte Naturtopografie, auch wenn der Realismus der Darstellung den Eindruck einer solchen evoziert. In *I'm Coming Home In Forty Days* bleibt hingegen alles im Bereich des Konkreten, das auf nichts anderes verweist außer auf das, was man sieht. Wesentlich näher als der deutschen Romantik mit ihrer zur Symbollandschaft transformierten Natur steht der Film deshalb den formalen Bildkonstrukten des Abstrakten Expressionismus. Insbesondere deren Affinität zum Konzept des Erhabenen scheint im Anblick des Eisbergs immer wieder durch. Erhaben nannte Kant ja jene Empfindung, die aus der Unbegrenztheit eines Gegenstandes resultiert, die Erfahrung des Betrachters an seine Grenzen führt, und ihn durch das alle vertrauten Erfahrungen Überschreitende in seinem Urteilsvermögen schlicht überfordert. Nun ist der eigentliche transzendentale Inhalt dessen, was Kant das Erhabene nennt, das Unvermögen zur Synthese, das zumindest in der Interpretation Jean-François Lyotards gerade die Künstler der Moderne durch Abstraktion hervorzubringen versuchten.[15] Die formale Reduktion und der dezidierte Purismus des Minimalisten unter den Abstrakten Expressionisten, Barnett Newman, steht demnach ganz im Dienst der Vergegenwärtigung des Absoluten mit der Transzendenz der Unmittelbarkeit. In seinem Text *The Sublime is Now*[16] behauptet Newman selbst programmatisch, die europäische Kunst befasse

15 DAS IST ZUMINDEST JEAN-FRANÇOIS LYOTARDS INTERPRETATION DER KRITIK DER URTEILSKRAFT, DIE AUS DER VON KANT GEFORDERTEN "NEGATIVEN DARSTELLUNG", DEM PARADOX EINER DARSTELLUNG, DIE NICHTS DARSTELLT, EINE ANKÜNDIGUNG DER ABSTRAKTIONISTISCHEN UND MINIMALISTISCHEN KUNST FOLGERT, EINER KUNST, "DURCH DIE DIE MALEREI DEM FIGURATIVEN GEFÄNGNIS ZU ENTKOMMEN VERSUCHT." JEAN-FRANÇOIS LYOTARD: *PHILOSOPHIE UND MALEREI IM ZEITALTER IHRES EXPERIMENTIERENS*. BERLIN 1986. S. 18.

16 BARNETT NEWMAN: *SELECTED WRITINGS AND INTERVIEWS*. ED. JOHN P. O'NEILL. BERKELEY. UNIVERSITY OF CALIFORNIA PRESS. 1990.

sich allein mit der Transzendenz des Gegenständlichen, die amerikanische hingegen, die sich vom Ballast der europäischen Traditionen befreit habe, strebe nach einem in sich selbst evidenten Bild, das real, konkret sowie universell verständlich sei und die Wirklichkeit der transzendentalen Erfahrung selbst zur Anschauung bringe. Der Abstrakte Expressionismus präsentiert sich so gesehen als Geschichte ontologischer Reduktion, an deren Ende allein das optische System der Bildfläche steht. Dieses Bild handelt nicht von einer Erfahrung, es will eine Erfahrung sein: Das Erhabene ist jetzt. Die ästhetische Präsenz des Farbraums ist sein Inhalt, d.h. das Bild präsentiert die Präsentation[17] und produziert, was sich in ihm ereignet. Der damit verknüpfte Anspruch einer völlig autonomen, nicht instrumentalisierbaren Kunst allerdings verweist auch auf einen metaphysischen Überbau, der in der Überzeugung resultiert, dass Authentizität allein auf einzigartiger, unmittelbarer ästhetischer Erfahrung beruht. Deshalb bestand das eigentliche Ziel Newmans auch darin, den Betrachter im Akt seiner Wahrnehmung zu isolieren, einer Wahrnehmung, die Newman sowohl mit dem Zeitempfinden selbst als auch der sublimen Augenblicklichkeit der emotionalen Erfülltheit verband. Die Konfrontation mit dem Werk ist demnach nichts anderes als der erfüllte Augenblick, der nicht der meßbaren Zeit, dem Chronos, sondern dem subjektiven Zeiterleben und Bewusstsein des Kairos gleichzusetzen ist. Diese Erfahrung impliziert die Idealkonstruktion eines aktiven Sehens, das die Wahrnehmung außerhalb der Grenzen von Kultur und Sprache situiert. Im Gegensatz zur gegenständlichen Welt des Scheins behaupten die Bildflächen Newmans letztlich, einzig für die immaterielle, geistige Welt der reinen, zeitlosen, unveränderlichen Begriffe und Ideen zu stehen. Dennoch erzielen seine Werke auch nach Abflauen der postmodernen Hochkonjunktur des Erhabenen eine abstrakte Wirkung, denn was auch immer metaphysisch in ihnen zur Darstellung kommt,

17 VGL. EBD., S. 15.

basiert auf einer präzisen physischen Form. Diese Form, die vor allem von der Dimension des Bildträgers bestimmt ist, umschließt den Betrachter im Großformat des Farbraums, und definiert einen präzisen Ort. In dieser räumlich strukturierten Interaktion von Bild und Betrachter, der Analyse der räumlichen Bedingungen von Malerei, liegt denn auch der eigentliche Anknüpfungspunkt für aktuelle künstlerische Positionen, die sich jenseits der spirituellen Dimension des Abstrakten Expressionismus verorten. Als a-historische, von kunstexternen Kontexten abstrahierende Auseinandersetzung mit Fragen der Sichtbarkeit, der Phänomenologie des Bildes und der Rolle des Betrachters kann Newmans Malerei so auch zur Referenz werden, wenn es um die veränderten Bedingungen der Visualität im heutigen Medienzeitalter geht. Die historisch motivierte Forderung nach strikter Trennung zwei- und dreidimensionaler Medien, von Malerei und Skulptur, jedenfalls scheint Vergangenheit, wenn die Frage nach dem Ort in der Malerei, dem abstrakten Farbraum, umgedeutet wird zur Frage nach dem Ort der Malerei an sich.

In diesem Sinne begegnet einem in *I'm Coming Home In Forty Days* zwar ein Insistieren auf das Jetzt der Wahrnehmung ähnlich wie bei Newman, das jedoch eine Erweiterung in Richtung jener minimalistischen Ästhetik findet, in der der Verweis auf die transzendentale Gegenwärtigkeit als Referenzsemantik in der objekthaften Präsenz aufgehoben ist. Der Erhabenheitsmodus artikuliert sich jetzt als Wahrnehmungsbedingung, die die Dauer verleihende Materialität auflöst zugunsten des Momenthaften ihrer jeweiligen aktuellen Erscheinung. Das zeigt sich deutlich in der letzten Einstellung des Films, die die Perspektive radikal umkehrt und eine monochrom grüne Fläche zeigt, die wirkt wie ein Standbild, tatsächlich aber das Wasser über dem Eis in direkter Aufsicht wiedergibt, so dass es als plane, undurchdringbare Oberfläche erscheint. Dieser Abstraktionsgrad dispensiert den Betrachter scheinbar von einer Suche nach einer außerbildlichen Referenz. Trotzdem evoziert die tableauartige

Einstellung eine ins Äußerste reduzierte Topografie des Sichtbaren, die sich in jener der Malerei sich annähernden Phänomenologie des Eises spiegelt, die ein Immer-wieder-neu-Wahrnehmen provoziert. Bei näherer Betrachtung wird nämlich ein leichter Strudel erkennbar, der die glatte grüne Fläche des Wassers durchzieht und als andeutungsweise wahrnehmbare Reflexion die Statik letztlich bricht.

Durch dieses Moment der minimalen Bewegung stellt die monochrome Fläche einen ablesbaren Raum dar, das heißt, sie ist mit Realität durchsetzt und kann einem Objekt zugeordnet werden. In Realzeit aufgenommen wird das Bild des Wassers vom Live-Bild zunächst scheinbar in ein Standbild transformiert, bevor die strukturierte Oberfläche dieser Optik eine materielle Qualität zuweist, die aus dem statischen Bild ein Bild in der Zeit werden lässt. Die grüne Fläche markiert quasi die Peripetie der Bewegung im Stillstand. Damit findet sich in ihr auch die für den Abstrakten Expressionismus konstitutive Dialektik von Prozessualität und Abgeschlossenheit mit ihren auf die räumliche Dimension sich öffnenden Farbflächen vergegenständlicht. Es ist das charakteristische Phänomen von Flächigkeit und Tiefe mit seinem wahrnehmbaren Übergang von materieller Oberfläche in immaterielle Bildfläche und fiktive, ideale Räumlichkeit, das hier als Sich-Verlieren in Farbe zur Anschauung kommt. Jetzt geht es allein noch um die grundlegende Trilogie von Sehen, Erkennen und Wiedererkennen in der Erscheinung. Auch der aus gefilterten Originalgeräuschen erstellte Soundtrack, der den vor Ort präsenten Ton auf einen minimalistischen Sound reduziert, fällt bei dieser letzten monochromen Einstellung weg. Als kontrapunktische Vereinigung aller Töne in der Stille lenkt er die Aufmerksamkeit allein auf das, was sich nicht erklären will jenseits seiner Sichtbarkeit.

VISION IN MOTION

Der bislang letzte Film *Of Three Men* (1998) ist das Konzentrat aus allem Vorherigen, die Reduktion auf das Maximum jenseits der üblichen "less is more"-Ästhetik. Auf 35 mm gedreht, präsentiert er sich als ungeschnittene 10-Minutenaufnahme, die in völlig statischer Einstellung einen Innenraum zeigt. Damit ist der kinematografische Apparat auf seine minimalste repräsentative Funktion reduziert. Durch die statische Ausrichtung der Kamera wird die Zeit direkt an den Faktor Licht und indirekt an den Faktor Belichtung gebunden. Veränderungen sind solche des Augenblicks, die immer nur rückblickend sichtbar werden, wenn die Gegenwart bereits Vergangenheit ist. Film fixiert und konserviert die Zeit als vergangene, im Prozess der Projektion jedoch wieder vergegenwärtigte, sowie den Blick als Blick des Kameraauges, der im Blick des Zuschauers reaktiviert wird. Wie auch immer die Formen der Zeit also konjugiert werden, sie treten stets allein im reduktionistischen Modus des Augenblicks in Erscheinung.[18] *Of Three Men* meditiert in diesem Sinne über Zeit und Raum, vor allem aber über das Licht als Materialisierung der Zeit in seinen Texturen, als Illumination, transzendente Erscheinung und gegenstandskonstituierende Substanz. Daneben steht die statische, durch den Lichtstrahl des Projektors konzentrierende Dunkelheit, die das Licht zur Bedingung des Sich-Offenbarens der Welt als Repräsentation erhebt.

Am Anfang ist konsequenterweise nichts zu sehen außer projizierter Dunkelheit; *Of Three Men* beginnt scheinbar als Repräsentation der bloßen Materialität des filmischen Trägers, als gesättigte, opake Fläche und auf die schwarze Projektion reduziertes Bildfeld. Doch der Signifikant spricht auch aus diesem dem Nicht-Bild sich annähernden Schwarz, wenn aus der negierten Abbildhaftigkeit sich schemenhaft die Konturen von Körpern entwickeln, bis klar wird, dass es sich um jene im Titel angesprochenen drei Männer handelt, die direkt vor der Kamera stehen und den Blick auf das Dahinterlie-

18   VGL. ONFRAY: *DIE FORMEN DER ZEIT*, A.A.O., S. 108.

gende buchstäblich verstellen. Wenn sie zur Seite treten, öffnet sich wie bei einem Bühnenvorhang der Blick in den Innenraum einer romanischen Kirche im inszenierten "fiat lux" als Grundbedingung visueller Wirklichkeitswahrnehmung.

In der Romanik präsentierte sich das Sonnenlicht in christlicher Instrumentalisierung nicht nur als Illumination, sondern auch als "lux perpetua", als ewiges Leuchten und Erleuchtung. Im umbauten Raum der Kirche herrscht eine flächig-räumliche Auffassung von Licht, die sich in den großen Glasfenstern und ihrer Modulation der Architektur manifestiert. Das Durchscheinen des "göttlichen" Lichts, das "Durchdringen des Lichts durch die Wände", die Diaphanie, wurde quasi als sensuelles Ereignis inszeniert, die den Kircheninnenraum vom Profanen trennt und im Spiel der Farben und des Lichts den Raum in das Symbol eines Raumlosen auflöst. Noch heute trägt das Licht ganz unabhängig von seiner funktionalen Vereinnahmung fast zwangsläufig die Konnotation des Transzendenten.[19] Der Raum in *Of Three Men* ist jedoch keine Kirche mehr, sondern eine Moschee. Bänke, Altäre und Sakralgegenstände sind verschwunden, der Boden ist mit Teppich bedeckt, und von der Decke hängen kitschige Kandelaber. Völlig zentralperspektivisch aufgenommen, richtet sich der Blick der Kamera auf die Kiblawand, die die Gebetsrichtung

---

19 DIESE SUBLIME SYMBOLKRAFT CHRISTLICHER IKONOGRAFIE, DIE SICH IM LICHT ENTMATERIALISIERT, SCHREIBT SICH ALS SÄKULARISIERTE ÄSTHETIK LETZTLICH NOCH IN DEN ARTIFIZIELLEN LICHT-RÄUMEN DES MINIMALISMUS FORT. DIE LICHTSKULPTUREN EINES DAN FLAVIN ODER JAMES TURRELL, IN DENEN DAS LICHT KONKRET UND ABSTRAKT, ABER AUCH IN SEINER METAPHYSISCHEN QUALITÄT ERSCHEINT, EVOZIEREN AUF ANDERER EBENE EINE VERGLEICHBARE WIRKUNG. FLAVINS POSITION, MIT EINFACHEN, INDUSTRIELL GEFERTIGTEN, GENORMTEN LEUCHTKÖRPERN LICHT ALS EREIGNISHAFTES PHÄNOMEN ZU INSZENIEREN, STEHT MIT DER VERWENDUNG DES UNSCHEINBAREN MATERIALS UND DER LOGISCHEN STRENGE SEINER ARCHITEKTONISCHEN ANORDNUNG ZWAR IM KONTEXT DER MINIMAL ART, DIE METAPHYSISCHE DIMENSION DES LICHTS KÖNNEN SEINE ARBEITEN TROTZ ALLER ENTWICKLUNG IN RICHTUNG EINER ENTSUBLIMIERTEN NICHT-KUNST, WIE SIE DIESEM REDUKTIONISTISCHEN MINIMALISMUS INNEWOHNT, JEDOCH NICHT VOLLSTÄNDIG ELIMINIEREN.

nach Mekka markiert. Diese befindet sich, wo früher das Eingangs-
portal war. Dort findet sich auch die Fensterrose, durch die helles
Licht fällt. Die Raumsituation der streng auf den Altar fluchtenden
Sakralarchitektur ist jedoch durcheinander geraten. Seitlich sind
zwar die Kreuzgänge zu sehen, diese haben ihre richtungsdefinie-
rende Funktion aber verloren, da die Raumstruktur der Moschee
sich im Gegensatz zu den auf den axial ausgerichteten christlichen
Sakralbauten durch die Gleichwertigkeit der Achsen und Himmels-
richtungen definiert.

In der filmischen Repräsentation von *Of Three Men* präsentiert sich
die zur Moschee transformierte Kirche als kulturelle Hybridfigur,
als pragmatischer Umgang mit dem Bestehenden, das einem neuen
religiösen Kontext angepasst wurde, ohne den christlichen Ursprung
des Baus zu negieren. Das liegt daran, dass die islamische
Moschee in erster Linie ein Betraum ist; sie ist kein eigentlich gehei-
ligter Raum, in dem die Gegenwart des Göttlichen als Vorstellung
lebendig ist. Fläche erscheint in islamischen Bauten als reine Fläche,
auch wird der Raum nicht von seinen Grenzen her bestimmt,
sondern definiert sich als Ort ohne vorgegebene symmetrische
Gesamtordnung, ohne Zentrum oder Fluchtpunkt. Diese dezentrale
Struktur der Moschee wird von der monokularen Zentralperspektive
der Kamera jedoch wieder in die abendländische Tradition des statischen Perspektivraums und sein Verständnis des Sehens gezwungen.[20] In der Konstruktion der Perspektive seit der italienischen
Renaissance befindet sich der intendierte Betrachter als Subjekt
des konstruierten Bildes im Fluchtpunkt der Sehlinien. Dieses per-
spektivische Konstrukt des Sehraums erweitert den Bildraum in

20 VGL. NORMAN BRYSON: *VISION AND PAINTING. THE LOGIC OF THE GAZE*. LONDON 1983. ZUR AFFINITÄT
ZWISCHEN DER MONOKULAREN PERSPEKTIVKONSTRUKTION UND DER APPARATIVEN OPTIK DER KAMERA
VGL. DIE ARGUMENTATION VON FILMTHEORETIKERN WIE CHRISTIAN METZ, JEAN BAUDRY UND STEPHEN
HEATH. VGL. ZUSAMMENFASSEND KAJA SILVERMAN: "WHAT IS A CAMERA?. OR: HISTORY IN THE FIELD OF
VISION". IN: *DISCOURSE*. 15.3. SPRING 1993. S. 3-38.

einen Raum vor dem Bild, in dem der Betrachter jene ideale Position findet, in der die Diskrepanz zwischen Bildproduktion und Realitätseindruck suspendiert scheint zugunsten der aktuell sich konstituierenden Wirklichkeit des Bildes. Zentralperspektive und Bildsymmetrie figurieren in *Of Three Men* somit als referentieller Bezug auf bildnerische Vorstellungen einer geometrischen Ordnung des Sichtbaren, in der die Konventionalität der Perspektive ein statisches, monokulares Verständnis des Sehens voraussetzt. Raum- und Wirklichkeitserfahrung bewegt sich ausschließlich innerhalb dieses präformierten Systems, das als instrumentelles Medium der Wahrnehmung funktionalisiert wird.

In der realistischen Malerei wie im Film basiert die idealistische Auffassung der Wahrnehmung auf einem plan-perspektivischen Blick, der als Bedingung einer überzeugenden Reduplikation der Welt figuriert. Die Logik dieses Blicks besteht darin, den Körper des Bildproduzenten wie des Betrachters auf einen einzigen Punkt auf der Netzhaut des Auges zu reduzieren und dadurch das Erfassen der Leinwand außerhalb jeder Zeitdauer zu situieren. Als punktueller Augen-Blick steht dieser idealisierte Blick für den hypothetischen Versuch, aus dem Kontinuum des Sehens wie der Zeit einen Moment der Bewegungslosigkeit zu isolieren. Damit entspricht er der apparativen Optik der Kamera, die als Substitut des Subjekts dessen Sicht präformiert, das Auge an das Objektiv delegiert und als Projektion des Selbst und Okkupation der Welt durch das Ich ganz der cartesianischen Logik des alles sehenden, zentralisierten Subjekts verpflichtet ist. Imaginär ist der Betrachter in der Perspektivkonstruktion immer schon im Bild, denn er befindet sich im Mittelpunkt des wirklichkeitsreproduzierenden Artefakts. Der Akt des Sehens wird dadurch in seiner Dauer ebenso negiert wie das Bewußtsein für die Zeit der Bildproduktion. Einer solchen "Metaphysik der Präsenz" [21] im Dienst der Illusion von Realität widerspricht

21 BRYSON: *THE LOGIC OF THE GAZE*, A.A.O., S. 89FF.

jedoch die faktische Beweglichkeit des sehenden Auges, das sich in seiner punktuellen Fokussierung immer nur auf einen Teil des Bildes konzentrieren kann. Im Gegensatz zu dem Konstrukt des alles auf einmal erfassenden Blicks, der das gemalte/filmische Bild zur Gegenwärtigkeit erhebt, vollzieht sich dieses Sehen nicht im Augenblick, sondern in der Dauer des Betrachtens.

Of Three Men reduziert den Innenraum der Moschee auf seine zentralperspektivische Ansicht, gibt dem Blick jedoch die Dauer des Sehens zurück. Das Kameraauge bleibt statisch, doch das Auge des Betrachters hat endlos Zeit, die Projektion zu studieren. Bewegung und Entwicklung werden zwar durch eine Reihe konzeptueller Bedingungen kontrolliert (Kamerastandpunkt, Zeit der Aufnahme), die Zeit selbst wird jedoch aus ihrer Verdinglichung der Präsenz befreit. Damit kehrt *Of Three Men* zu den Anfangstagen der Filmgeschichte mit ihrer feststehenden Kamera zurück: kein Bewegungsbild, sondern ein Bild in Bewegung, das sich weniger durch seinen Zustand als durch seine Tendenz auszeichnet.[22] Allein das sich verändernde Licht artikuliert sich als Bewegungsintensität und Extension im Raum. In dieser minimalen Bewegung des Bildes, das die Kamera reproduziert, liegt die eigentliche Herausforderung des filmischen Prinzips, wenn sich innerhalb seiner dispositiven Struktur ein überaus sinnliches Gemälde konstituiert, das in der Zeit existiert.

Die Moschee präsentiert sich im Medium Film als leuchtende wie belichtete Architektur, ein skulpturaler, sein Licht extern empfangender Projektionsraum. Als Skulpteur des Lichts steigert er dieses in seiner Effizienz, lenkt, kontrolliert und formt es. Allein das durch das Rundfenster im Mittelpunkt des Bildes einfallende Licht lässt sich als direkte Lichtquelle lokalisieren; das durch die seitlichen Fenster strömende Sonnenlicht hingegen präsentiert sich als ereignishaftes Phänomen. Indem es beiläufig an die ständige Transition der Realität

22 VGL. DELEUZE: *DAS BEWEGUNGS-BILD*, A.A.O., S. 43F.

erinnert, verwandelt dieses Licht die Moschee auch in ein Wahrnehmungsmodell, das den Sinn für Proportion und für das Sehen selbst verändert. Denn letztlich ist die Isomorphie zwischen der Struktur des Raums und jener der Wahrnehmung so angelegt, dass Wahrnehmungsmuster der alltäglichen Erfahrung gerade keine Wiederholung finden, sondern gebrochen werden durch die Sehgewohnheiten verletzende Umstrukturierung des Raums. Das Innere steht in Abhängigkeit vom Außen, was auch bedeutet, dass das, was zu sehen ist, Folge dessen ist, was nicht zu sehen ist. Veränderung ist allein abhängig von den externen Lichtverhältnissen, die das Andere im aleatorischen Bereich des Besonderen inszenieren. Bewegung entsteht allein aus der Veränderung des einfallenden Lichts, aus der Veränderung der Schatten, Texturen, selbst der schwindenden Dreidimensionalität der Dinge. Das Licht in seiner Doppelcodierung von *Lux* und *Lumen*, physikalischem und metaphysischem Licht, ist so gesehen transzendentale Bedingung der sinnlichen Vorstellung, der ästhetischen Repräsentation und Voraussetzung sowohl des Sichtbaren in seiner Sichtbarkeit als auch seiner Abbildung. Es schließt immer auch ein Verhältnis zur Dunkelheit als seiner Negation ein, zu der es sich als Intensität definiert. In seiner konstanten Veränderung ist das Licht aber auch Repräsentation der Zeit, jener Zeit, die sich als realistische, unsichtbare, von jedem Sinn befreite Sphäre des raumzeitlichen Kontinuums hinter dem Schein der unzerstörbaren Dauer verbirgt.

Die Zeit des Lichts ist zirkulär, da sie durch den Lauf der Sonne bestimmt und induziert wird. Wenn diese hinter einer Wolke hervorscheint oder dahinter verschwindet, gibt es jedoch eine quantitative wie chromatische Modifikation, die auch die Wahrnehmung des Raumes und seiner Gegenstände betrifft, und damit die sich verändernden Lichtverhältnisse zum Maß und zur Evidenz der vergehenden Zeit erhebt. Die Witterung ist die sichtbare, immanente und ästhetische Variation der regelmäßig und zirkulär verfließenden Zeit. Als meteorologische Form der Zeit durchkreuzt sie deren Kontinuum.

Im Rhythmus von Tag und Nacht kehrt alles mit einer kalkulierbaren Regelmäßigkeit wieder, die Teil einer Logik ist, die keine Wahrscheinlichkeit kennt, sondern von Gewissheiten lebt. Die meteorologische Zeit hingegen ist rein aleatorisch und moduliert Licht und Schatten in unvorhersehbarer Weise.[23] In *Of Three Men* materialisiert sich allein in den farbigen Variationen des Lichts die Zeit zur Sichtbarkeit. Wenn die zirkuläre Zeit also durch die aleatorische Zeit visualisiert wird, bedeutet das auch, dass die Textur der ersten nichts anderes ist als die Expansion der zweiten.[24]

Die Ontologie der Zeit zeugt aber auch davon, dass diese verwandelt, verlangsamt, modifiziert und geformt werden kann. Obschon sie sich definieren lässt als das irreversible Verhältnis eines Nacheinanders, wird sie objektiv und subjektiv unterschiedlich wahrgenommen. Als gedachte muss die Zeit artifiziell verräumlicht werden, um zur Sichtbarkeit zu gelangen, als erlebte hingegen artikuliert sie sich außerhalb chronometrischer Strukturen. Im Film wird Zeit primär als Bewegung erfahren, als Abfolge distinkter, am Auge vorbeiziehender Momente. Der Film vollbringt das Paradox, sich der Zeit des Objekts anzupassen und gleichzeitig noch einen Abdruck von dessen Dauer vorzunehmen.[25]

De Rijke/de Rooij verlangsamen das Tempo zur "real time" und bringen in der Parallelschaltung von Wahrnehmungszeit und Aufnahmezeit das Gesehene in der Reproduktion erneut zur Wahrnehmung. Dadurch lösen sich ihre Filme von der Realitätshaftigkeit der Einstellung als Block homogener Zeit, den André Bazin noch zum Garanten jenes Realismus erklärte, der die Ontologie des filmischen Bildes bestimmt. Statt dessen entsteht eine kaum aufzuhebende Differenz

---

23 UND WEIL DAS WETTER SO UNVORHERSEHBAR IST, IST DER LICHTEINFALL IN DIE MOSCHEE AUCH KEIN VOLLKOMMEN NATÜRLICHER, SONDERN EIN WENIG MANIPULIERT – FILMISCHE REKONSTRUKTION ZU DEN BEDINGUNGEN MÖGLICHST NATÜRLICH ERSCHEINENDER KÜNSTLICHKEIT.

24 VGL. ONFRAY: *DIE FORMEN DER ZEIT*, A.A.O., S. 51FF.

25 VGL. BAZIN: *QU'EST-CE QUE C'EST LE CINÉMA?*, A.A.O., S. 151.

zwischen subjektivem Zeitempfinden und der Zeit des Films, bei der die Erfahrung von Zeit im Fluss der Bilder niemals die der eigenen Erfahrung der Zeit im Realen ist. Das ist eigentlich paradox, denn *Of Three Men* ist ein Film in Realzeit, dessen Dauer von zehn Minuten exakt zehn Minuten gefilmter Zeit entspricht. Doch der Blick auf das Medium ist so konditioniert auf dessen eigene temporale Realität aus Beschleunigung und Verlangsamung, dass gerade die Modifikationen des Lichts als indexikalische Repräsentation der Zeit eine extreme Verlangsamung der realen Zeit suggerieren. *Of Three Men* hat seinen eigenen Rhythmus, der von unserem differiert, gerade weil er eigentlich nur das Tatsächliche in ein anderes Medium übersetzt. Doch die Zeit in *Of Three Men* ist eine meditative Zeit, während unsere eine chronografische ist. Diese unaufhebbare Differenz spielt bei der Rezeption eine wesentliche Rolle, da die Zeit im Film nicht mehr die des Ereignisses ist, sondern die der ästhetischen Erfahrung. Ästhetische Erfahrung vollzieht sich im Modus präsentischer Kontemplation, bei dem das Ereignishafte innerhalb der ästhetischen Zeit sich nicht zwangsläufig referentiell zu den Ereignissen der Realzeit verhält.

Solche die Ewigkeit der Zeit als Inszenierung ästhetischer Erfahrung präsentierende "real time movies", in denen die Kamera statisch auf ein Objekt gerichtet ist, rufen natürlich Andy Warhols *Empire* ins Gedächtnis, jener 8-stündige Stummfilm über das New Yorker Empire State Building, in dem sich nichts ereignet außer den minimal sich verändernden Lichtverhältnissen, der einsetzenden Dunkelheit und der künstlichen Beleuchtung des Wolkenkratzers. Aus der 44. Etage eines gegenüberliegenden Gebäudes aufgenommen, zeigt Warhols Film lange Zeit das Empire State Building in fast unveränderter Ansicht, bis das Art-Deco-Monument aus Glas und Stahl nach Sonnenuntergang in Dunkelheit und Bedeutungslosigkeit versinkt. Das flächige Bild aus Licht und Dunkel verliert am Ende vollständig seinen referentiellen Bezug zur Wirklichkeit und transformiert sich scheinbar in die reine Materialität des Filmbildes. In seiner epischen Länge und dem konsequenten Verzicht auf jegliche Intervention außer der Wahl des Kamerastandpunkts ist *Empire* die absolute Hommage an die Zeit als reine Dauer, an das irreduzible Verfließen von Zeit. Trotz seiner obsessiven Fixierung auf das Gebäude handelt Empire jedoch ebensowenig von diesem wie von der abstrakt chronometrischen Zeit. In seiner Reduktion auf das allein Sichtbare ersetzt er Chronologie und Geschichte konsequent durch den Prozess des Zusehens, denn hinter dem sichtbaren Bild des Wolkenkratzers gibt es kein unsichtbares, das plötzlich hervortreten und den Dingen retrospektiv die ersehnte Bedeutung verleihen könnte. *Empire* setzt vielmehr einen sich als Bildausschnitt definierenden Rahmen, hinter dem es keine andere Wirklichkeit gibt: der absolute Rahmen des Bildes als Materialität ohne Substanz.

In dieser radikalen Herausforderung des Kinos als Ort der Geschichten, der Zerstreuung und des Spektakels hat Warhol dem Film ein ontologisches Terrain erschlossen, in dem dieser, von jeder Figurativität abstrahierend, das eigentliche Medium ästhetischer Erfahrung bildet. Allein in ihrer simplen Dauer verändern Warhols Endlosfilme die Wahrnehmung, die darauf wartet, dass etwas passiert, dann aber die Unveränderlichkeit des Bildes eintauscht gegen die Perspektive der minimalen Veränderung des de facto Gleichen.[26] In dieser Absolutsetzung der Dauer gegenüber der chronologischen Zeit orchestriert der Film die Temporalisation der Betrachtung und Aufmerksamkeit des Blicks als Fixierung auf die Wahrnehmung an sich: Das Betrachten der Filme Warhols wird zum endlosen Betrachten des eigenen Zusehens. Das ist eine radikale Absage an das Bemühen der Kinematografie, die Oberflächlichkeit des Bildes aufzulösen zugunsten der vorgeblich dahinter liegenden Wirklichkeit, und dabei die Zeit des Sehens als Decodierung seiner Zeichen zu negieren. Der Reiz der Aufhebung der räumlichen Dimension mit ihrer geometrischen Perspektivität liegt insofern in der Aufhebung der Zeit in der Dauer, im Austausch der Zeit der Vernunft gegen die Zeit der

Intensität. Zeit wird zur qualitativen Dauer, wenn die räumliche und zeitliche Dimension eine Gleichzeitigkeit erhalten, die intuitiv wahrgenommen werden kann. Dieser intuitive Eindruck zeitlicher Dauer artikuliert sich als Kontinuität des Fließens, die nur als einheitliche, nicht als sukzessive Abfolge distinkter Momente erfahren werden kann. Die wahrgenommene Wirklichkeit selbst verwandelt sich hier in reine Bewegung, in der keine starren Dinge existieren, sondern "allein werdende Dinge, keine Zustände, sondern nur Zustände, die sich verändern."[27]

In *Of Three Men* gibt es allein die Bewegung im Raum als Bewegungsintensität des Lichts. Der Innenraum der Moschee präsentiert sich tatsächlich als Momentaufnahme jenseits dezidiert konzeptueller Überlegungen, eine abstrakte Idee in eine vorgefertigte Dramaturgie zu übersetzen. Als bloße Affirmation des Raums und der Phänomenologie seiner sinnlichen Erscheinung kennt *Of Three Men* keine Finalität; alles könnte ewig so weiter gehen. So gesehen zeigt er nichts anderes als zehn Minuten aus dem Kontinuum der Zeit und des Lichts – und damit nichts anderes als die Ontologie des Filmischen in ihrer reinsten Form.

26 WARHOLS FILME WIE *EAT* (1963, 29 MIN.), *SLEEP* (1963, 321 MIN.), *KISS* (1963, 50 MIN.) ODER *EMPIRE* (1964, 485 MIN.) ZEIGEN ALLEIN DAS, WAS DER TITEL BENENNT: JEMAND ISST, JEMAND SCHLÄFT, LEUTE KÜSSEN SICH. DIE URSPRÜNGLICHE HERAUSFORDERUNG DIESER ÜBERLANGEN FILME LAG IN IHRER VORFÜHRUNG ALS KINOFILM – WAS MACHT DAS PUBLIKUM, DAS ERWARTUNGSFROH IM KINOSESSEL SITZT, WENN ES AUF DER LEINWAND IMMER NUR DAS FAST GLEICHE ZU SEHEN GIBT? NEBEN DIESER VON WARHOL INTENDIERTEN REZEPTION DES BETRACHTENS ALS HAPPENING, ZU DEM DER FILM NUR DEN ANLASS UND SPÄTER DEN VISUELLEN SOUNDTRACK LIEFERT, STEHT JEDOCH DIE ÄSTHETISCHE EIGENGESETZLICHKEIT DES FILMISCHEN MATERIALS, DIE DEN ANLASS ZU EINER ANALYSE DER FILMISCHEN ZEIT BIETET, DIE VÖLLIG UNABHÄNGIG VOM KINOKONTEXT IST. WARHOLS FILME FUNKTIONIEREN DESHALB AUCH PERFEKT IM AUSSTELLUNGSKONTEXT, WIE NICHT ZULETZT DOUGLAS GORDON MIT SEINER BOOTLEG EMPIRE VERSION GEZEIGT HAT, DIE ALS HOMMAGE AN WARHOLS WERK DIESES IN DEN REZEPTIONSKONTEXT KUNST RÜCKT UND DAS TEMPORALE MOMENT DER BETRACHTUNG MIT DER KATEGORIE DES ÄSTHETISCHEN VERBINDET.

27 HENRI BERGSON: *DENKEN UND SCHÖPFERISCHES WERDEN*. FRANKFURT/M. 1985. S. 211.

POSTMINIMALE PROJEKTIONEN
(INSIDE AND OUTSIDE THE FRAME)

Die Verbindung des Genres der Malerei mit dem des Kinos, wie
de Rijke /de Rooij es praktizieren, strebt weder danach, das Ideal
einer neuen kinematografischen Intermedialität zu behaupten, noch,
in der Synthese verschiedener Ästhetiken die Entdifferenzierung der
Künste zu forcieren. Auch geht es nicht darum, den Charakter des
filmischen Mediums zu verallgemeinern. Hinter den Arbeiten von de
Rijke /de Rooij steht vielmehr die Einsicht, dass der filmische Apparat
ein Nebeneinander ästhetischer, diskursiver wie technischer
Faktoren darstellt, der für verschiedene Artikulationsformen offen ist.
Film als Kunst, jener das Medium seit seinen Anfangstagen beherr-
schende Gedanke, wird von ihnen in eine neue Form überführt,
wenn sie die Kunst nicht im Dispositiv Kino aufgehen lassen, sondern
im Gegenteil ihre Filme explizit im Kontext institutionalisierter Kunst
präsentieren und damit in ein diskursives Umfeld stellen, das andere,
außerfilmische Kriterien als referentiellen Rahmen setzt.

Eine dieser Referenzen manifestiert sich als Erbe des amerikani-
schen Minimalismus bzw. postminimalistischer Zugriff auf das
Wirkliche als Parameter der Wahrnehmung von Zeit und Raum.
Verbunden damit ist auch die Implikation von *Anwesenheit*, die für
die Operationsfelder der bildenden Kunst zunehmend an Bedeutung
gewonnen hat. Ausgehend von der Minimal Art der späten sechziger
Jahre, die das Verhältnis von Werk und Betrachter sowie die Über-
schneidung von Zeit, Raum und Bewegung einer formalistischen
Redefinition unterzog, rückte deren Konzept von "presence and
place" ins Zentrum künstlerischer Praxis.[28] Durch die dezidierte Posi-
tionierung der minimalistischen Objektkunst wurde dem Betrachter
der souveräne Raum der klassischen Kunst verweigert zugunsten
des Hier und Jetzt der Präsenz des Werks. Die auf jede Referenz
außerhalb ihrer selbst verzichtenden Werke der Minimal Art evozierten

---

28 VGL. GEORG STEMMRICH (HG.): *MINIMAL ART – EINE KRITISCHE RETROSPEKTIVE.* DRESDEN / BASEL
1997. S. 12.

so ein Präsenzerlebnis neuer Art, bei dem die kategoriale Bestimmung der Plastik umfunktioniert wurde auf Verhaltensweisen des Betrachters, die als solche nur möglich waren, wenn eine Kontinuität des Raumes bestand, in dem sich Objekt und Rezipient gleichermaßen befanden. Dabei ging es nicht mehr nur formalistisch um die Oberfläche des Werks als Ausdruck seiner medialen oder materiellen Eigenschaften, sondern auch um eine Erkundung der wahrnehmbaren Konsequenzen seiner Intervention innerhalb eines bestimmten Raums.[29] In der Konfrontation mit den Objekten des Minimalismus war der Betrachter praktisch gezwungen, auch ein Bewusstsein für die eigene Physikalität im Verhältnis zum Kunstwerk zu entwickeln. Im Gegensatz zu phänomenologischen Konzepten der Sichtbarkeit war es in der Minimal Art allerdings immer die materielle Struktur des Objekts, die als konzeptuelle Basis der Visualität diente und dem Betrachter ein Bewusstsein seiner Position im Sichtbaren liefern sollte. Dieser musste in der Reflexion der Zeitkomponente in der Wahrnehmung den Koordinaten von Zeit und Raum im Umgang mit dem Werk einen exponierten Stellenwert zugestehen. Auf diese Weise setzte der Minimalismus Fragen der Zeit in der Kunst selbst frei, die dem Verständnis des Modernismus und namentlich des Abstrakten Expressionismus mit seiner Vorstellung des Kunstwerks als gegenwärtig und auf einen Blick erfassbar

---

29 DER AMERIKANISCHE MINIMALISMUS BRICHT MIT DER TRADITION DES IDEALISMUS, AUCH WENN ER DIE REINE FORM UND LOGISCHE STRUKTUR AFFIRMIERT ODER ABSTRAKTEN GEDANKEN EINE FORMALE GESTALT VERLEIHT. DENN ES IST GERADE DER METAPHYSISCHE DUALISMUS VON SUBJEKT UND OBJEKT, DEN DER MINIMALISMUS IN DER PHÄNOMENOLOGISCHEN ERFAHRUNG DES WERKS ZU ÜBERWINDEN SUCHT. INSOFERN VERKOMPLIZIERT DAS MINIMALISTISCHE WERK DIE REINHEIT DES KONZEPTS DURCH DIE KONTINGENZ DER WAHRNEHMUNG. LETZTLICH STREBT DIE VON DER MINIMAL ART AUSGEHENDE ANALYSE MEHR ZUR EPISTEMOLOGIE ALS ZUR ONTOLOGIE, DENN SIE RICHTET SICH EHER AUF DIE BEDINGUNGEN DER WAHRNEHMUNG UND DER GRENZEN DER KONVENTION INNERHALB DER KUNST ALS AUF DEREN FORMALE ESSENZ UND KATEGORIALES WESEN. VGL. HAL FOSTER: "DIE CRUX DES MINIMALISMUS". IN: G. STEMMRICH A.A.O., S. 599FF.

diametral gegenüberstanden, da der transzendentale Moment kategorisch ersetzt wurde durch die Dauer der Betrachtung.

In der konzeptuellen Dichotomie von Materialität und Visualität rückte insofern auch die Frage nach einer Neuverortung der Kunst im Sichtbaren ins Zentrum, eine Frage, die über das historische Paradigma der Minimal Art hinaus noch immer Aktualität besitzt.[30]

In der postminimalistischen Kunst lebt dieser Aspekt trotz des diversifizierten Charakters der künstlerischen Produktion und Verabschiedung der Kohärenz der Form zugunsten pluraler Konzepte unter modifizierten Vorzeichen fort – Zeit und Raum sind nach wie vor bestimmende Parameter vieler Werke sowohl auf semantischer als auch materieller Ebene.

In seiner formalen Analyse der Wahrnehmung, der Konfrontation von "bekannter Konstante und erfahrener Variation" (Robert Morris), war der Minimalismus zudem eine Auseinandersetzung mit den Wahrnehmungsbedingungen als Dissoziation von Wahrnehmung und Wissen in der Reduktion auf konkrete Parameter. Vor allem dieses Interesse an der Verschränkung der Repräsentation des vermeintlich Bekannten mit seiner Wahrnehmung als Unbekanntes teilt er mit dem den eigenen apparativen Status reflektierenden Film. Denn auch die cineastische Erforschung künstlerischer Praxis in der Tradition des autoreflexiv strukturalen, aber auch des konzeptuellen Kinos befragt indirekt Wahrnehmungsformen nach ihrer Modellierung durch Bildformen. Mit der Art, wie Film die Welt abbildet, repräsentiert er sich geradezu als Syntax zum Verständnis der Welt, das heißt, das Interesse am Bild ist auch eine der filmischen Logik verpflichtete Neuformierung des Realen, die sich trotz aller Abstraktion noch immer innerhalb der Paradigmen des Pikturalen bewegt.

Die Arbeiten von de Rijke/de Rooij nun zeichnen sich durch die Tatsache aus, dass sie trotz eines spezifischen räumlichen Interesses

---

30 VGL. EBD., S. 29.

sowie der Schaffung definierter Umgebungen als solche so gut wie keine Materialität besitzen, denn als Film bestehen sie vor allem aus projiziertem Licht im Raum. Indem sie strukturell auf Zeit und Raum insistieren, rekonfigurieren diese Arbeiten jedoch das Rohmaterial der raum-zeitlichen Parameter.

Vor allem auf semantischer Ebene tritt das Bewusstsein für die Dimensionen als Determinanten jeder kinematografischen Illusion deutlich hervor und artikuliert sich als Prinzip: Raum und Zeit sind in den Arbeiten von de Rijke/de Rooij geradezu plastisch sichtbare Kategorien. Darin liegt ein entscheidender Unterschied zum konventionellen Film, der sich selbst als Gegenstand in der vollständigen Referenzillusion aufzuheben und dadurch auch in seiner Materialität zu negieren sucht. Diese negierte technisch-apparative Dimension des filmischen Bildes gelangt bei de Rijke/de Rooij, die einen präzisen Modus des Betrachtens fordern, hingegen deutlich zur Sichtbarkeit. Indem sie die von der Kinoleinwand übernommene Funktion des Rahmens durch das innerbildliche Framing ersetzen und ihren Film nicht auf Leinwand projizieren, sondern direkt auf die weiße Wand, zielen sie auf eine imaginäre Trennung von Apparatur und Bild. Allein die Wandfläche um das projizierte Bild herum formt einen Rahmen, der es gegen die Architektur des Raums abgrenzt. Zwischen dem das Wirkliche mimetisch wiedergebenden Gemälde, dem Schein des Bildes und dem Materiellen seiner Funktion bleibt immer eine optische Differenz. Beim Filmbild hingegen fehlt diese erkennbare Differenz zwischen Bildstoff und Bild, selbst wenn das Bildfeld der Leinwand der Projektion eine gewisse objekthafte Qualität verleiht. Das führt einerseits zu einer Dematerialisierung der lichthaften Projektion, der bei de Rijke/de Rooij noch zusätzlich das Passepartout des begrenzenden Kinovorhangs fehlt, andererseits aber auch zu einer Materialisierung des gesamten "white cube", der nicht allein Umraum, sondern konkreter Ort des filmischen Bildes ist. Dieser Raum, der kein Kino simulieren will, aber dessen konzentrierende Atmosphäre übernimmt, minimiert die dispositive Vergegenständlichung des filmischen Diskurses, betont andererseits aber auch die materielle Struktur des filmischen Apparats, gerade weil er neben der referentiellen Dimension der Repräsentation sichtbarer Wirklichkeit auch den essentiellen Charakter von Film als projiziertem Licht-Bild in die Präsentation integriert. Der externe Rahmen der Filme von de Rijke/de Rooij präsentiert sich als Hybridfigur, die die formale Struktur des Kinos mit den Raumintervention der minimalistischen Skulptur verbindet. Auch wenn der Film nicht projiziert wird, existiert der Raum, zu dem er gehört. Denn neben dem Faktor der Zeit, der das Medium Film von allen anderen materiellen Künsten unterscheidet, ist es vor allem das unabdingbare Ende der Projektionszeit, das ihn zu einem konzeptuellen Konstrukt erhebt, bei dem die Abwesenheit des Bildes und Erinnerung an das gerade Gesehene auch die Zeit nach seiner aktuellen Präsenz in den Rahmen des Werks mit einschließt. Die Ästhetik des Verschwindens verwandelt die immaterielle Substanz des Licht-Bildes zwangsläufig in eine verblassende Erinnerung; in seiner Einprägung jedoch überdauert das Bild als Spur im Gedächtnis.

Im Rahmen seiner Kontextualisierung im System Kunst erhält das substantielle Moment des Kinematografischen, der zeitliche Rahmen der Projektion, insofern einen expliziten Stellenwert. Als analoges Bildmedium besitzen die Arbeiten von de Rijke/de Rooij eine präzise zeitliche Definition, die nicht zuletzt durch die ontologische Bedingung des Films, einen Anfang und ein Ende zu haben, bestimmt wird. Sie werden nicht als Endlosschleife projiziert, sondern als in sich abgeschlossene Vorführung, die – siehe Aushang – in bestimmten Intervallen ihre Wiederholung findet. So fordern das Werk und seine Betrachtung ihre eigene Zeit, die das Publikum sich gezwungenermaßen nehmen muss.

Neben dem Rekurs auf minimalistische Positionen in Bezug auf die Form der Präsentation als Rahmen des Films positioniert sich jedoch auch dieser selbst in einem Rahmen aus der Kunst adaptierter

Referenzen. Insbesondere die formalen Regularien der Malerei und der Bezug zu anderen "time-based arts" bestimmen die Ästhetik der Arbeiten von de Rijke/de Rooij.

Das filmische Medium präsentiert sich in ihnen deshalb sowohl unter dem Aspekt seiner materiellen Spezifität als auch dem des von ihm ausgehenden perzeptiven Potentials. Indem das Narrative des Films direkt an die materiellen Bedingungen filmischer Bedeutungsproduktion rückgebunden wird, tritt der mimetische Diskurs des Kinos in die Sphäre des selbstkritischen Diskurses der Moderne. Doch diese Gegenüberstellung von filmischer Realität und der Selbstreferentialität modernistischer Visualität ist nur ein Aspekt unter vielen, der vor allem die beiden ersten Filme, *Chun Tian und Forever and Ever*, betrifft. Diese partizipieren zumindest noch marginal am Raster filmischer Narration, wenn auch weniger auf thematischer als auf formaler Ebene, das heißt, sie präsentieren keine handlungsgeleitete Thematik, sondern eine filmische Struktur, die das eigentliche Thema erst produziert, und sei es nur im Leerraum zwischen den Bildern. Die Gegenstandslosigkeit des Themas führt zur Thematisierung der Form, der Bewegung und der Wahrnehmung des Realen im Illusionsraum des Films. Dabei darf jedoch nicht außer Acht gelassen werden, dass filmische Repräsentation nicht allein von Wahrnehmungsdispositionen präfiguriert ist, sondern auch den Regularien einer historisch sanktionierten Ästhetik unterliegt. Wenn das Medium Film als technische Erzeugung von Bildern einer näheren Betrachtung unterzogen wird, rückt die Auseinandersetzung mit der Dialektik von Film und apparativer Optik dezidiert in den visuellen Referenzrahmen der Malerei.

Ein solcher Rekurs auf die Malerei als Paradigma einer Bestimmung des Visuellen ist vor allem aufschlussreich, insofern er den Film auf jene pikturalen Traditionen zurückzuführen sucht, in denen er sich als Bildmedium bewegt, gegen die er sich aber auch ästhetisch abgrenzen will. Schließlich ist es gerade die Anwendung visueller

Kompositionsprinzipien auf die filmische Gestaltung und die Interferenz der Regularien des statischen und der des bewegten filmischen Bildes, die eine mediale Differenz zwischen traditioneller und technischer Bilderzeugung hervorbringen, die nicht allein produktionsästhetisch motiviert ist, sondern sich auch auf die Relation von apparativen Bedingungen und verschiedenen Formen des Sehens bezieht. Das bedeutet allerdings nicht, dass sich der Transfer des aus der Kunst gewonnenen Erkenntnispotentials allein in einem selbstreferentiellen Diskurs vollziehen muss, der die Differenz von Perzeption und Apperzeption zum *issue* erhebt. Auf der Suche nach der Malerei begegnet der Film vielmehr auch seinen eigenen Grundlagen, die ihn als technisch-apparatives Medium zur Bilderzeugung nicht zwangsläufig an die Spitze modernistischer Ästhetik befördern. Obschon den ästhetischen Diskurs der Malerei der Moderne der grundlegende Verzicht auf illusionistische Raumtiefe und den zentralperspektivischen Fluchtpunkt der Renaissance charakterisiert, zeichnet sich das narrative Illusionskino ja gerade durch die Aktivierung der klassisch illusionistischen Mittel zur Erzeugung räumlicher Strukturen aus. Der narrative Film strebt geradezu nach dreidimensionaler Raumwirkung als Negation der tatsächlichen Flächigkeit des Filmbildes zugunsten des Realitätseindrucks. Rahmen und Tiefenschärfe, die als Strukturierung der Repräsentation auf jene Darstellungskonventionen der klassischen Malerei verweisen, die durch die moderne Kunst gebrochen wurden, bilden primäre Funktionen seines formalästhetischen Repertoires. Während der Verzicht auf dargestellte Raumtiefe in der gegenstandslosen Malerei konsequent zur Thematisierung von Flächigkeit geführt hat, fiel das Medium Film so gesehen ziemlich anachronistisch hinter die ästhetischen Errungenschaften des Modernismus zurück.[31] Erst mit seiner Ausdifferenzierung als die Konvention durchbrechendes, selbstreflexiv auf filmischer Metaebene operierendes Medium gewinnt der Film sein vom bloß Abbildhaften abstrahierendes Potential im Kontext künstlerischer Produktion und Rezeption. Das meint nicht allein die

Instrumentalisierung der Kinematoie als Reflexionsmedium künstlerischer Praxis oder die Abkehr von der Repräsentation des Wirklichen in der Auflösung des filmischen Bildes in die grafische Oberfläche.

In den Arbeiten von de Rijke/de Rooij wird die Rhetorik des Films vielmehr erneut an die Malerei angeschlossen, um deren Komponenten von Format, Proportion, Perspektive und Komposition einer erneuten Befragung zu unterziehen. Dabei bleibt ihr Zugriff auf die Realität durchaus phänomenologischer Natur; die sichtbare Realität erscheint zwar als von malerischer Tradition präformiertes Bild, es gibt jedoch keine direkt kunsthistorisch motivierten Rekurse auf die Malerei oder auf wiedererkennende Lesbarkeit abzielende Zitate. Einzelne Einstellungen werden zwar wie Gemälde behandelt, die tableauhaften Einstellungen erschöpfen sich jedoch nicht darin, dass sie bestimmte Analogien zur pikturalen Gestaltung aus dem Archiv der Kunst aufweisen. Deren historische Errungenschaften, zum Ausgangspunkt des Films erhoben, machen diese komponierten Einstellungen vielmehr gerade zu Produkten dessen, was sie nicht sind. De Rijke/de Rooij rekurrieren allein auf ein abstraktes Gerüst, das sie aus den historischen Bildraumerfindungen, aber auch den monochromen Farbräumen des Modernismus destillieren. Es sind deshalb der oft symmetrische Bildaufbau, der Einsatz von Plan-Tableaux und die starre Kamera mit ihrer Zentralperspektive und Bildsymmetrie, die als referentieller Bezug auf bildnerische Vorstellungen einer geometrischen Ordnung des Sichtbaren figurieren und auf die Systematisierungen des Visuellen seit der Renaissance mit ihren bildnerischen Regularien etwa der Perspektivkonstruktion verweisen.

Das Potential einer subjektiven, personifizierten Kamera lassen die Filme von de Rijke/de Rooij völlig außer Acht; ihre systematisierende

---

31 VGL. YVONNE SPIELMANN: "FRAMING, FADING, FAKE: PETER GREENAWAYS KUNST DER REGELN".
IN: JOACHIM PAECH (HG.): *FILM, FERNSEHEN, VIDEO UND DIE KUNST*. STUTTGART 1994. S. 132–149.

Betrachterposition bleibt immer an eine klar definierte ästhetische Grenze gebunden. Auch das Bildfeld ist bei ihnen ein geometrisches, ein geschlossenes System entlang ausgewählter Koordinaten. In diesen Raumkompositionen aus Horizontalen und Vertikalen finden alle Bewegungen einen festen Halt; die geometrische Konzeption des Bildfeldes liefert einen vorgegebenen Rahmen für all das, was sich narrativ in ihn einschreiben wird.[32] Überdies tritt die Distanzierungsfunktion des Rahmens immer wieder im Filmbild selbst in Erscheinung, als innerbildliche Duplizierung durch geometrische Strukturen oder architektonische Konfigurationen, die neue Bildausschnitte im eigentlichen Bildausschnitt setzt.[33] Als Betonung eines Abstands, der bereits durch die auf die Beschreibung von Vertikalen reduzierte Kameraführung produziert wird, löst auch dieses Moment der sichtbaren Bildgrenze die Differenz zwischen Filmbild und Tafelbild punktuell immer wieder auf.

Der Rahmen des Gemäldes umschließt einen Raum, der eine nach innen gerichtete, zentrifugale Orientierung aufweist. Das filmische Tableau hingegen ist von einer Maske umschlossen, die sich durch das Moment der Bewegung als virtuell nach außen hin offene Sichtschranke präsentiert.[34] Dieser vom Kameraausschnitt erzeugte Bildrahmen figuriert als Begrenzung des Raumes und nimmt Klassifikationen wie Strukturierungen des Realen vor. Die Bildbegrenzung

---

32 VGL. GILLES DELEUZE: *DAS BEWEGUNGS-BILD. KINO 1.* FRANKFURT/M. 1989. S. 28F. MIT SEINER GRUNDSÄTZLICHEN DIFFERENZIERUNG ZWISCHEN GEOMETRISCHEM UND PHYSIKALISCHEM BILDFELD. DAS GEOMETRISCHE BILDFELD DEFINIERT, WAS SICH IN IHM BEWEGT, DAS PHYSIKALISCHE HINGEGEN PRÄSENTIERT SICH ALS DYNAMISCHE KONSTRUKTION, DIE IN DIREKTER ABHÄNGIGKEIT VON DER SZENE UND DESSEN PERSONEN WIE OBJEKTEN KONZIPIERT WIRD.

33 IN IHREN FILMEN GIBT ES IMMER WIEDER INNERBILDLICHE ÄSTHETISCHE GRENZEN IN FORM SICHTBAR INS BILD GEFÜGTER RAHMEN WIE DAS VERTIKALE BALKONGITTER IN *FOREVER AND EVER* ODER ABER DAS PLÖTZLICH IM BILD AUFTAUCHENDE GELÄNDER DER SCHIFFSRELING IN *I'M COMING HOME IN FORTY DAYS*.

34 VGL. ANDRÉ BAZIN: "PEINTURE ET CINÉMA". IN: *QU'EST-CE QUE LE CINÉMA. ÈDITION DÉFINITIVE.* PARIS 1981. S. 188.

bedeutet also das Finden eines Rahmens, der jenen Ausschnitt definiert, der als Bild der Kamera und der Projektion figurieren soll. Normalerweise versucht das filmische Bild jedoch zu negieren, dass es einen Rahmen besitzt, wenn es sich als das Reale selbst ausgibt. Es ist bestrebt, im Fragmentarischen des Ausschnitts das Viele zu repräsentieren, und mit dem sich selbst verleugnenden Ausschnitt die Wirklichkeit mit der Omnipotenz des Blicks zu inszenieren. Der begrenzende Rahmen, will er nicht an die Malerei erinnern, lässt den Prozess der Ausschnittfindung im Resultat des Filmbildes verschwinden oder aber erhebt den Bildrand selbst zum Funktionsträger, der über das aktuelle Bild hinaus in das darauffolgende als sichtbar Unsichtbares verweist.

Dieser zentrifugale, virtuell nach außen gerichtete Bildaufbau wird in den filmischen Konstruktionen von de Rijke/de Rooij indessen von der sichtbaren Setzung des Ausschnitts als begrenzendes Raster immer wieder in Frage gestellt. In solchen, auch auf höherer Ebene nicht aufhebbaren Antagonismen, tritt das System des Bildes als Regulativ der Repräsentation plastisch hervor. Durch die extrem langen Einstellungen ihrer Filme treten noch zusätzliche Parameter hinzu, die die Aufmerksamkeit von dem Sichtbaren auf das Unsichtbare, jenes hinter dem strukturierten Raum befindliche unstrukturierte Ganze verlagern, durch die sich das filmische Bild als konstruiertes Artefakt zu erkennen gibt. Dadurch wird auch evident, dass der Raum als Terrain des geometral-aneignenden Sehfeldes nur als optische Illusion einer zweiten Dimension existiert. Film beschränkt sich, abgesehen von der Tonspur, die bei de Rijke/de Rooij sowieso nicht im Dienste eines filmischen Realismus steht[35], auf die wahrnehmbaren Eigenschaften der Dinge, die im Zustand der Entmaterialisierung präsentiert werden, wenn sie sich verwandelt haben in reine Sichtbarkeit ohne Substanz.

Doch es gibt noch eine andere, zunächst vielleicht gegenläufig erscheinende Kategorie, die als abstrakte Qualität die Ästhetik ihrer Filme bestimmt, und das ist das eigentlich kinematografische

Moment der Zeit. Film besteht zwar aus unzähligen Einzelbildern, doch seine Erscheinungsform ist die jenes Kontinuums, das auch das des Sehens ist. Darin differiert er signifikant von der Fotografie wie der Malerei, in denen die Zeit konzentriert ist im Augenblick des Stillstands. Die Fotografie isoliert einen Moment des Realen aus dem Fluss der Zeit, während die Malerei in Bezug auf den ihr eigenen Modus der Repräsentation einen kategorial anderen Begriff der Dauer entwickelt. Auch wenn immer die Rede vom filmischen Bild ist, ist dieses deshalb im eigentlichen Sinne gar kein Bild, in dem das stillgestellte Kontinuum der Zeit seinen Ausdruck findet. Film entwickelt sich im Gegenteil erst aus der Negation des Bildbegriffs als statisches Konstrukt. Film nutzt nicht nur das Mehr, das er gegenüber dem Bild als Abstraktion der Sinne besitzt, sondern auch die Zeit in ihrer Materialisation in der Bewegung. Seine eigentlich plastische Tiefenwirkung gewinnt der Film in der Zeit; die Zeit selbst wird von ihm als Perspektive reproduziert.[36]

Was nun die Filme von de Rijke/de Rooij charakterisiert, ist allerdings gerade die Reduktion der cineastisch manipulierten Bewegung; in ihnen findet (fast) alles in *real time* statt. Vor allem in ihren letzten beiden Arbeiten – *I'm Coming Home in Forty Days* und *Of Three Men* – konstituiert sich das Filmische primär aus der sichtbaren Differenz zu jenen anderen Bildern, die sich in der Zeit eben nicht ändern.

35 IN KEINEM DER FILME VON DE RIJKE / DE ROOIJ GIBT ES EINE DIREKT DIEGETISCHE VERBINDUNG VON BILD UND TON, IN VIELEN FÄLLEN SOGAR ÜBERHAUPT KEINEN TON, ALLENFALLS DIALOGE UND GERÄUSCHE AUS DEM OFF, DIE NUR IMAGINÄR DEM AKTUELL SICHTBAREN ZUGEORDNET WERDEN KÖNNEN. CHUN TIAN KENNT NUR STIMMEN AUS DEM OFF, EBENSO *FOREVER AND EVER*, IN DEM DAS ENERVIERENDE KLINGELN EINES TELEFONS EINE ZENTRALE ROLLE SPIELT, OHNE DASS DAS TELEFON JEMALS ZU SEHEN IST. WENN AM ENDE DES FILMS DIE PERSONEN SICHTBAR SPRECHEN, IST DAS FAST SCHON IRRITIEREND. IN *I'M COMING HOME IN FORTY DAYS* IST DER TON RADIKAL HERUNTERGEFAHREN UND DIE REALE GERÄUSCHKULISSE ZU EINEM MINIMALISTISCHEN SOUNDTRACK MONTIERT; *OF THREE MEN* BEGINNT MIT ÜBERLAUTEN GERÄUSCHEN, UM FAST TONLOS ZU ENDEN.

36 VGL. DELEUZE: *DAS BEWEGUNGS-BILD*, A.A.O., S. 42.

Diese Differenz zwischen statischem und bewegten Bild ist
normalerweise in einer Evidenz formuliert, dass sie erst gar nicht
wahrgenommen wird, wenn die Affinität zum statischen Bild eine
semantische und keine strukturelle ist, die in der Permutation
der beschleunigten Zeit wieder von anderen, "filmischen" Bildern
überlagert wird.

Auch und gerade angesichts der Allgegenwart medialer Bilder stellt
sich deshalb die produktive Frage, was denn überhaupt ein Bild ist,
immer wieder neu. Dabei sind es die medialen Bilder selbst, die in
ihren filmischen Codes den eigenen Status im Feld des Sichtbaren
indirekt immer reflektieren. Diese im Darstellungsprozess bewirkte
Verschiebung und Verdichtung des Wirklichen findet bei de Rijke /
de Rooij allerdings nicht digital per Video statt, sondern klassisch
analog. Dadurch steht in den von ihren Filmen repräsentierten,
abstrakten Wirklichkeitsmodellen auch die spezifische Qualität eines
traditionellen Mediums als Bildmodell zur Diskussion. Der analoge
Film als Garant einer halbwegs existenten Referenz an ein vorgängiges
Original steht im Gegensatz zum digitalen Videobild, das konnotativ
mit einer Flüchtigkeit versehen ist, die ihr Pendant in der Vorstellung
der Qualität der Dauer findet, die der Film dem Gesehenen angeblich verleiht. Rein materiell fixiert der Film das Wahrgenommene
tatsächlich in einem stärkeren Maße als das Video, auch in besserer
Bildauflösung. Video hingegen gilt als Medium, das auch sichtbar
machen kann, was eigentlich nicht sichtbar ist – durch Verlangsamung oder Beschleunigung der Bilder, durch Vergröberung des
Rasters, Überlagerung und Umkehrung, Phasenverschiebung und
die digitale Nachbehandlung des apparativ Fixierten. Video objekti-
viert die Illusion des Sichtbaren in dem Maße, wie seine elektroni-
schen Bilder ihre Manipulierbarkeit und das Unentschiedene, Nicht-
Authentische fast schon voraussetzen.

Zu den Grundvoraussetzungen des Dispositivs Kino hingegen gehört,
dass das filmische Bild das Reale selbst zu sein scheint, dass es,
wie Roland Barthes formuliert, ein "perfektes Analogon" zur

Wirklichkeit bildet.[37] Der monokulare Kamerablick simuliert nicht die Wirklichkeit, sondern die Position des Subjekts. Der Glaube an den Schein der Realität als das Reale selbst muss deshalb zumindest vorhanden sein, damit der Film das Kriterium des Abbildhaften erfüllt. Dieser Schein des Analogons führt andererseits aber auch zur Thematisierung des Sehens an sich, denn Film ist nicht das radikal Andere der Wahrnehmung, sondern eingebunden in das, was visuelle Wirklichkeitserfahrung ihrer Struktur nach ist. Film repräsentiert in diesem Sinne das Andere im Selben als Besonderheit einer Dekonstruktion von Blick und Bild.[38] Im kinematografischen Prozess der Abbildung, in der (Re-)Produktion des Analogons als apparatives Erscheinen, findet etwas statt, das die außerfilmische, "reale" Seherfahrung als Blick- und Bildgewissheit einer permanenten Befragung auf ihren Realitätsgehalt unterwirft, aus der diese Seherfahrung nie ganz unbeschadet hervorgeht. Film dekonstruiert unseren Begriff von Realität, indem er ihn in die Bahnen des Metonymischen lenkt, wo allem Gezeigten einen Augenblick lang die vertraute Signifikanz verloren gegangen ist. Film verspricht Realität und transportiert doch nur eine Möglichkeit der Wirklichkeit im selektiven Blick der Kamera. Das weiss man, doch die Verführung des Kinos setzt alles daran, dieses Faktum vergessen zu machen zugunsten des Stiftens jenes Realitätseffekts der symbolischen Ordnung, in dem das Leinwandgeschehen seine Legitimation findet. In diesem Paradox einer Nähe durch Distanz können Film und Zuschauer immer nur eine imaginäre, weil nie tatsächlich erreichbare Einheit bilden, deren Basis der referentielle Bezug zur Wirklichkeit ist.

Allerdings löst das filmische Bild in der Realitätsverdoppelung das Konzept von dieser einen Wirklichkeit genauso auf, wie es in seiner

37 ROLAND BARTHES: "DIE FOTOGRAFIE ALS BOTSCHAFT". IN: *DER ENTGEGENKOMMENDE UND DER STUMPFE SINN. KRITISCHE ESSAYS III.* FRANKFURT/M. 1990. S. 13.

38 VGL. MICHAEL KÖTZ: *DER TRAUM, DAS SEHEN UND DAS KINO. FILM UND DIE WIRKLICHKEIT DES IMAGINÄREN.* FRANKFURT/M. 1986, S. 91FF.

Wirkungsweise den Raum durch die Hereinnahme der Zeit auflöst. Das Bildfeld lässt sich zwar mit dem Realen ein, zwingt dieses aber zu einer eigentümlichen Koexistenz mit seinem filmischen Double und erzeugt eine Konfiguration, in der das Reale und seine technische Verdoppelung nicht mehr nur wie bei der Fotografie referentiell, sondern auch zeitlich und damit strukturell aneinander gekoppelt sind. Unter Berücksichtigung der kinematografischen Verstellung im Realen, in dem die Oberfläche der Dinge nicht zeigt, was die Dinge sind, sondern allein wie sie wahrgenommen werden, beschäftigen sich de Rijke/de Rooij deshalb mit der Kinematografie im engeren Sinne, der Bildbegrenzung, Kameraperspektive, Tiefenschärfe, Kamerabewegung, der Architektur und Beleuchtung.

Weil das Medium in seiner kategorialen Doppelwirklichkeit unmittelbar mit der Darstellung verknüpft ist, gilt ihr Interesse der Differenz zwischen Film und Realität, dem Verlust der Dreidimensionalität, dem begrenzten Bildfeld und der Montage, dem Fehlen akustischer und anderer Sinneseindrücke. Über diese Differenz setzen sie die filmische Reproduktion in direkte Spannung zur reproduzierten Wirklichkeit, wenn allein der Modus der Abbildung zur ästhetischen Intervention im Feld des Sichtbaren wird.

Mit der Integration der formalen wie semiotischen Distanz in die filmische Repräsentationsstruktur nähern sich de Rijke/de Rooij andererseits auch der konkreten Form des Objekthaften, die Film als Film in seiner ästhetischen Zeichenhaftigkeit transparent erscheinen lässt. Ihr filmischer Diskurs (denn Film ist immer Welt transformiert in Diskurs) verlagern den Schwerpunkt auf die spezifische Wahrnehmung von Realität in ihrer medialen Transformation. Die materielle Spezifität des Films wird von ihnen deshalb nie ganz negiert, sondern in der visuellen Dekonstruktion jenes "Realitätseffekts" präsentiert, der nicht anderes meint als eine sich als Reales präsentierende Welt zweidimensionaler Bilder. Dass die objektivierende Macht der filmischen Apparatur im Gegensatz zu der Idee eines direkten

Zugangs zur Realität steht, wird geradezu zum ästhetischen Prinzip.
Das bedeutet auch eine Entfernung vom Primat des zu Sehenden
zugunsten einer Hinwendung zu dem wahrnehmenden Blick an sich.
Das Betrachten der Filme von de Rijke/de Rooij bleibt daher stets
ein bewusstes Betrachten von Bildern, wenn diese nur bedingt über
sich hinaus in die Welt verweisen, deren Repräsentation sie liefern.
Die Farben ihrer Filme sind irgendwie immer zu bunt oder zu flau,
jedenfalls scheinen sie nicht unmittelbar der Außenwelt entnommen,
obwohl sie auch nicht synthetisch wirken. Die Ausschnitte sind Bildausschnitte, die dem konventionellen Blick widersprechen, auch
wenn sie nicht direkt befremden. Dadurch erhält das Wirkliche eine
visuelle Substanz, die gerade aus der Differenz zu dem gewöhnlich
Sichtbaren ihr Potential gewinnt. Vorprogrammierte Wahrnehmungs-
fähigkeiten werden irritiert, aber die Verfremdung interveniert nur
geringfügig in Bezug auf das Wirkliche. Was sich viel stärker bemerk-
bar macht, ist der Effekt der Distanzierung und die Zeitlichkeit der
Wahrnehmung als zentrale Kategorie des Filmischen, die in einen
neuen Kontext der Befragung der Konditionen dieser Wahrnehmung
gerückt wird.

Selbst eine solche Anbindung des Films an die Kategorie der autonomen Kunst kann den Bedingungen des Kinematografischen
jedoch nur schwer entkommen: Die Ausrichtung der Betrachtung an
die am Kunstwerk orientierte, selbst/bewusste Rezeption und das
wesentlich an die Form gebundene reflektierende Sehen trägt bei
aller Abstraktion immer Restspuren jener Illusionsmaschine, die das
Wesen des Kinos bestimmt. Der Faszination der anderen Realität
erliegt man früher oder später doch.
In den Arbeiten von de Rijke/de Rooij gibt es deshalb ein wieder-
kehrendes formales Element, das diese Faszination des Filmischen
als sinnliche Qualität des wahrgenommenen Bildes in eine konzep-
tuelles Konstrukt überführt: Sie enden immer mit einem plötzlichen
Schnitt, einem unerwarteten Abbruch des Projekts "Film".

Dieses Ende verhält sich kontrapunktisch und – aus Perspektive des Publikums – kontraproduktiv zu dem eigentlichen Rhythmus der Bilder, den es abrupt unterbricht.

Als produktive Nichtbeachtung der Rhetorik der Finalität bewahren die Filme damit jedoch den Charakter des Fragmentarischen, das seine Vervollständigung erst in der leeren Wandfläche nach dem Ende der Projektion findet. Es ist diese konzeptuelle Leere als Bestandteil des Werks, die die Abwesenheit des Bildes zum positiven Bestandteil seiner selbst erhebt. Die Leere nach dem Ende des Films zu sehen bedeutet insofern auch, das in seine Wahrnehmung aufzunehmen, was in sie hinein gehört, aber abwesend ist, und damit die Abwesenheit des Fehlenden als Eigenschaft des Gegenwärtigen wahrzunehmen.

APPENDIX / ANHANG

BIOGRAPHY/BIOGRAFIE

Jeroen de Rijke
*1970 in Brouwershaven (NL)

Willem de Rooij
*1969 in Beverwijk (NL)

1990 -1995 Gerrit Rietveld Academie, Amsterdam
1997 -1998 Rijksakademie, Amsterdam

FILMOGRAPHY/FILMOGRAFIE

"Of Three Men"
(1998, 10 min, 35 mm colorfilm/Farbfilm)

"I'm Coming Home in Forty Days"
(1997, 15 min, 16 mm colorfilm/Farbfilm)

"Voor Bas Oudt"
(1996, 2 min, 16 mm colorfilm/Farbfilm)

"Forever and Ever"
(1995, 18 min, 16 mm colorfilm/Farbfilm)

"Chun Tian"
(1994, 3 min, 16 mm colorfilm/Farbfilm)

EXHIBITIONS (SELECTION)/AUSSTELLUNGEN (AUSWAHL)

2000 Museum of Art Yokohama, Yokohama (G/C)
Galerie Rüdiger Schöttle, München (E/S)
Stedelijk Museum Bureau, Amsterdam (E/S)
Kunsthaus Glarus, Glarus (E/S)
"Duration", Büro Friedrich, Berlin (F)
"Man muss ganz schön viel lernen, um hier zu funktionieren",
Frankfurter Kunstverein, Frankfurt am Main (F/C)
"Global positions", Der Standard, museum in progress, Wien

1999 "L'Autre Sommeil", Musée d'Art Moderne de la Ville de Paris,
ARC, Paris (G/C)
"h:min:sec", Kunstraum Innsbruck, Innsbruck (G)
Galerie Daniel Buchholz, Köln (E/S)
"To the People of the City of the Euro", Frankfurter Kunstverein,
Frankfurt am Main (G/C)
"Of three Men", Städtisches Museum Abteiberg,
Mönchengladbach (E/S/C)
Fri-Art, Fribourg (G/C)

1998 "Seamless", de Appel Foundation, Amsterdam (G/C)
Manifesta 2, Casino Luxembourg, Luxembourg (G/C)
"h:min:sec", Kölnischer Kunstverein, Köln (G)
Moderna Museet, Stockholm (F)
"Grown in Frozen Time", Shed im Eisenwerk, Frauenfeld, (G)

1997 "Verbindingen/Jonctions", Palais des Beaux Arts, Brussels (G)
26e International Film Festival, Rotterdam (F/C)
"Prix de Rome 96", Dordrecht Museum, Dordrecht (G/C)
IDFA (International Documentary Filmfestival), Amsterdam (F)

1996 "Timing", Stichting de Appel Foundation, Amsterdam (F)

1995 Nederlands Filmfestival, Utrecht (F/C)
"Double You Street 139", W 139, Amsterdam (F)

E = EINZELAUSSTELLUNG   S = SOLO EXHIBITION   C = CATALOGUE/KATALOG

G = GROUP EXHIBITION/GRUPPENAUSSTELLUNG   F = FILMVIEWING/FILMVORFÜHRUNG

BIBLIOGRAPHY/BIBLIOGRAFIE

Gerald Ichterhoff, "It is beautiful, isn't it?", in: *Texte zur Kunst*, Heft 37, März 2000.

Véronique Bouruet-Aubertot, "Zoom, Chemins de travers", in: *Beaux-Arts magazine*, Februar 2000.

Studio, Israel, Januar 2000.

"L'autre sommeil", in: *Atlantica*, Januar 2000.

Elisabeth Wetterwald, "L'autre sommeil", in: *Parpaings*, Januar 2000.

"L'autre sommeil", in: *aden, Le Monde*, 26. Januar 2000.

Phillippe Régnier; "Sommeil trompeur. Roni Horn et 'L'autre sommeil' à l'ARC", in: *Journal des Arts*, 7. Januar 2000.

Renate Roos, "Jeroen de Rijke/ Willem de Rooij", in: *Kunstforum International*, Bd. 148, Dezember 1999 - Januar 2000, S. 344.

Lex ter Braak, "Kalme eindeloosheid", in: Metropolis M, Nr. 6, Dezember 1999 - Januar 2000.

Angeline Scherf, "L'Autre Sommeil: The Other Sleep", in: *L'Autre Sommeil*, hrsg. von: Musée d'art moderne de la ville de Paris, Ausstellungskat., 17.11.1999 - 23.1. 2000, S. 77-80.

Carlos Basualdo, "Panic Desire", in: *L'Autre Sommeil*, hrsg. von Musée d'art de la ville de Paris, Ausstellungskat., 17. November 1999 - 23. Januar 2000, S. 91-99.

Heidrun Wirth, "Indien-Illusion", in: *Kölnische Rundschau*, 2. Oktober 1999.

Renate Roos, "Indische Impressionen - Vier Filmsequenzen 'Forever and Ever'", in: *Kölner Stadt-Anzeiger*, 30. September 1999.

Christian Huther, "To the People of the City of the Euro", in: *Kunstforum International*, Bd. 147, September - November 1999, S. 417-418.

Verena Auffermann, "Alle Ekstasen im Schrank - Das Innen nach außen: neue Ausstellungsstrategien in Frankfurt", in: *Süddeutsche Zeitung*, 10./11. Juli 1999.

Rudolf Schmitz, "Waschbeton hinter Dauerregenschleier", in: *Frankfurter Allgemeine Zeitung*, Nr. 129, 8. Juni 1999, S. 5.

S. Blomen-Radermacher, "Zeit sichtbar und spürbar machen", in: *Rheinische Post*, 3. Juni 1999.

Silke Hohmann, "Transparenz als Prinzip", in: *Journal Frankfurt*, 11.- 24. Juni 1999, S. 38.

"Film im Film. Rauminstallationen von de Rijke/de Rooij im Museum Abteiberg", in: *Mönchengladbach Aktuell*, 1. Juni 1999.

Vanessa Joan Müller, "Jeroen de Rijke und Willem de Rooij", in: *frankfurter kunstverein. Hefte 0/99*, Mai 1999, S. 13.

"A Fri-Art, trois Hollandais multiplient les sensations", in: *Der Bund*, 22. Mai 1999.

Sandra Danicke, "Der Raum und seine Ordnung 'To the People of the City of the Euro' im Kunstverein", in: *Frankfurter Rundschau*, Nr. 123, 31. Mai 1999

Michael Hierholzer, "Spiegelungen der Stadt im künstlichen Raum", in: *Frankfurter Allgemeine Zeitung*, Nr. 122, 29. Mai 1999.

Jost Martin Imbach, "Dichte Atmosphäre dank Farbe", in: *La Liberté*, 13. April 1999.

Heike Tekampe, "h:min:sec", in: *Kunstforum International*, Bd. 143, Januar - Februar 1999, S. 378 ff.

Lars Bang Larsen, "Off the silver screen", in: *Nu: - The Nordic Art Magazine*, Nr. 1/1999, S. 54-57.

Tanja Elstgeest, "The film rolls, a thought takes shape...", in: *Cross*, Nr. 2/1999, S. 123-129.

Arno Orzessek, "Auge, blick mal! Die Ausstellung 'h:min:sec' in Köln: Auf dem Höhepunkt des Tempos hält die Kunst die Uhr an", in: *Süddeutsche Zeitung*, Nr. 273, Dezember 1998, S. 14.

Jürgen Raap, "Entdeckung der Langsamkeit: 'h:min:sec' - eine Ausstellung mit cineastischen Highlights und Künstlervideos im Kölnischen Kunstverein", in: *Kölner Illustrierte*, Dezember 1998.

Sandra Smallenburg, "Open dagen voor jonge kunstenaars", in: *NRC Handelsblad*, 26. November 1998.

Georg Imdahl, "So lange es dauert - wem die Stunden, Minuten, Sekunden schlagen: Der Kölner Kunstverein nimmt sich die Zeit", in: *Frankfurter Allgemeine Zeitung*, Nr. 271, 21. November 1998, S. 38.

Claudia Posca, "Manifesta könnte Nachfolgerin der 'Biennale des Jeunes' werden", in: *Kunstforum International*, Nr. 142, Oktober-Dezember, 1998, S. 358.

Amine Haase, "Auch Gary Cooper lädt zur Zeitreise ein",
in: *Kölner Stadt-Anzeiger*, 23. Oktober 1998.

Kathrin Lutz, "Mitgegangen - Mitgehangen - Mitgefangen.
Die Manifesta in Luxemburg: Drei Kuratoren auf Identitätssuche",
in: *Noëma Art Journal*, Nr. 49, Oktober/ November 1998, S. 104-105.

Basil Nikitakis, "Plötzlich ist es 'Zwölf Uhr mittags'",
in: *Kölnische Rundschau*, 23. Oktober 1998.

Amine Haase, "Zwischen Eisberg und Kanalrohr, zwischen
Kunst und Kino: Udo Kittelmanns Schau 'h:min:sec'",
in: *Kölner Stadtanzeiger*, Nr. 247, 23. Oktober 1998.

Christoph Blase, "Luxemburger Pluralismus - Zur Manifesta 2",
in: *Kunst-Bulletin*, Nr. 9/1998, S. 16-21.

Jan Braet, "Manifesta 2", in: *Kunstbeeld*, September 1998.

Matthias Frehner, "Nachdenkliche junge Kunst zwischen Lift und Eis.
Manifesta 2 in Luxemburg", in: *Neue Zürcher Zeitung*, 7. Juli 1998.

Pierre Olivier Rollin, "Réalisme identitaire", in: *Le Matin*, 6. Juli 1998.

Mireille Descombes, "Manifesta 2: Une expo qui dit "je" ",
in: *L'Hebdo*, 2. Juli 1998.

Hans den Hartog, "Werkelijkheid als kunst op de Manifesta
in Luxemburg", in: *NRC Handelsblad*, 27. Juni 1998.

Manifesta 2 - Europäische Biennale für zeitgenössische Kunst,
Luxembourg, 28. Juni - 11. Oktober 1998, *Mini-Guide*, S. 63.

Maria Lind, "The Biography of an Exhibition",
in: *Manifesta 2*, Ausstellungskat., Luxembourg, 1998.

Martijn Verhoeven, "Films over Afstand en vervreemding",
in: *Seamless*, Ausstellungskat., 1998.

Sylvie Ferré et Henri-Michel Borderie, "Les jeunes nomades
"manifestent" à Luxembourg", in: *Inter- art actuel*, Nr. 71, 1998.

Hans den hartog Jager, "Werkelijkheid als kunst op de Manifesta
in Luxemburg", in: *NRC Handelsblad*, 27 Juni 1998.

Jorinde Seijdel, "Koud comfort",
in: *Het Financieele Dagblad*, 18. April 1998.

Edwin Carels, "Broedend Brussel",
in: *Metropolis M*, Bd. 18, Nr. 3, 1997, S. 46.

Lilet Breddels, "Prix de Rome 1996", Ausstellungskat.,
Amsterdam 1996, S. 78-79, 81, 100-105.

Ernst-Jan Rozendaal, "Beeldend kunstenaars per film",
in: *Provinciale Zeeuwse Courant*, 8. Juni 1996.

Hans Beerekamp, "Veel kunst om de Kunst bij eindexamens
Rietveldacademie", in: *NRC Handelsblad*, 28. Juni 1995.

TABLE OF ILLUSTRATIONS/ABBILDUNGSNACHWEIS